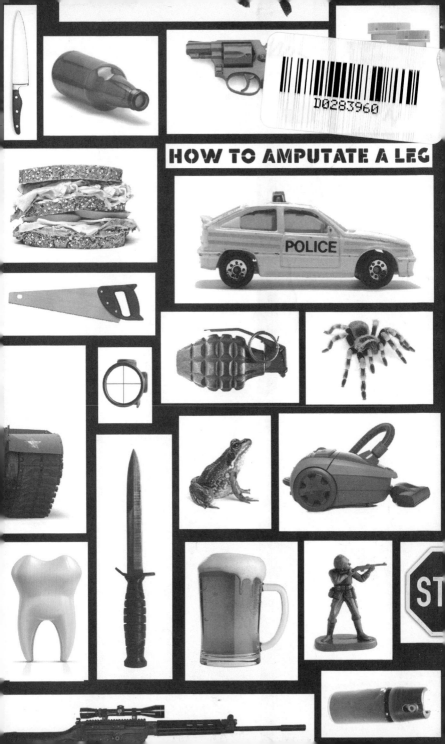

HOW TO AMPUTATE A LEG

HOW TO AMPUTATE A LEG

AND OTHER WAYS TO STAY OUT OF TROUBLE

NATHAN MULLINS

ALLEN&UNWIN

First published in 2009

Allen & Unwin
83 Alexander Street
Crows Nest NSW 2065
Australia
Phone (61 2) 84 25 01 00
   Fax (61 2) 99 06 22 18
Email info@allenandunwin.com
  Web www.allenandunwin.com

National Library of Australia Cataloguing-in-Publication entry:
Mullins, Nathan, 1972-
How to amputate a leg : and other ways to stay out of trouble
ISBN: 978 1 74237 037 8 (pbk.)
1. Mullins, Nathan
2. Adventure and adventurers—Anecdotes.
3. Adventure and adventurers—Biography.
920.71

Cover and text design by Bruno Herfst
Printed in Australia by McPherson's Printing Group

10 9 8 7 6 5 4 3 2 1

To Helen

*Your strength, passion, love, friendship,
unwavering support, bravery and the way you live life
have always thrilled and empowered me.
I have done nothing without you.*

CONTAINS

INTRODUCTION

There are a few things you should know

This is not a medical textbook

If you bought this book as a guide for amputating a leg, I'm sorry, go and return it. On the other hand, if you're the sort of person who thinks that is a skill you may need to employ sometime, then read on, I may have a few pearls for you anyway.

Thanks for reading this book. I should start by saying that I don't feel particularly qualified to write a book, but don't let that put you off. Also, I don't feel sufficiently aged to be in a position to pass on my accumulated knowledge. I always feel like 80-year-olds have that right, and few others. At 36 I have a fair way to go.

I will be upfront and say that I don't have a particularly auspicious academic record, no masters degrees, or, in fact, any type of degree, and I have not accumulated any massive amount of wealth which entitles me to call myself successful. I am an unremarkable athlete. I am an ordinary guy with a family and a house and all the regular commitments.

What I do have is experience.

I have been places and seen things. I have seen amazing human triumph, and terrible disasters, sometimes at the same place and time. I have been in danger and, if I'm honest, put other people in danger too. I have been lucky.

CHARITY WORK

I grew up in suburban Melbourne, in a normal family. I have a sense of social justice that has pushed me into certain fields. When I left school I started to work for a large trade union. That gave me a good look at sections of our community that I had never seen before, and an idea of what is fair. The people who worked at the union were really committed to social justice, and inspired me with their high ideals. I also got an amazing insight into state and federal politics, and was thoroughly enthralled and sometimes repulsed at the same time. I will always feel very fortunate for this grounding in social responsibility and intense snapshot of politics.

After a while I just wanted more. I didn't really know what, but more. I started to look towards the army for adventure and a sort of community service. I was not attracted to charity work in any way, though my family has a long tradition of this, but I wanted somehow to do my bit.

I joined the army and went straight to 2 Commando Company, 1st Commando Regiment. This was the Australian Army's reserve special forces and it was absolutely amazing. It was hard work, in a team of motivated, tough individuals, and incredibly rewarding. We trained and practised the huge array of skills the special forces soldier needs and routinely jumped out of planes and helicopters, swam through the blackened Southern Ocean, periodically walked through deserts and jungles carrying heavy packs, regularly climbed cliffs of rock and snow, and laughed all the time. I could not have picked a better unit to join. I remember the advertisement that got me in. It asked for guys who were fit, committed, tough, volunteer parachutists, comfortable in the ocean and mature. As a surfer, that sounded like me, except the mature bit.

The 1st Commando Regiment sent me all over Australia, and also to Brunei, Singapore and Papua New Guinea. I worked with soldiers from all over our region and served in a peace-monitoring force in PNG. It taught me to be resolute, to look past the obvious, to be aggressive when you need to be, and calm and easy-going the rest of the time. It taught me that I had huge power, but should be humble.

I spent the turn of the millennium in the jungle in PNG, on peace operations for the Australian Army, listening to bombs go off nearby. Local villagers were exploding old bombs that were lying around from World War II by placing them in their cooking fires. They reckoned it was a great way to ring in the year 2000. I bet you just used fireworks. How passé.

Unless you have been in such a unit, you are imagining the wrong thing about the army I was in. After twelve years of service I could count on one hand the number of salutes I had performed to officers. We didn't march around the barracks and I never spit-polished my boots, ever. My boots were for walking long distances in swamps or deserts, not the parade square. My rifle was for killing the enemy, not twirling around my arm like a trick monkey. We had no time to practise that crap, and no wish to either. You imagine that military units want people who are all the same; in the 1st Commando Regiment everyone was different. I came into the unit as a left-leaning unionist and political agitator while my best mate in the unit could easily have been a Nazi in a previous life. It worked though.

We used to look at the Melbourne skyline from 10 kilometres

offshore, treading water in the inky blackness of 2 AM Port Phillip Bay, and wonder what the rich people were doing. It couldn't be as amazing as what we were doing.

After a while I decided I needed a change and joined the Victoria Police. My brother was a detective at the time, and enjoyed 'the job', as it is colloquially referred to. I stayed as a reserve member of the Australian Army, but was a policeman as well. It was a great mix, with many complementary, if not directly applicable, skill sets. Again, I felt like joining the police was a sort of community service, with car chases thrown in as a bonus. (Car chases are easily as exciting as they seem in the movies.)

I worked in the western suburbs of Melbourne and enjoyed all the different situations that confronted a police officer every day. When you asked a question, people gave you an answer. When you told them to do something, they did it. If I'm honest, I also enjoyed the things about the police that would appeal to a little boy. Chasing crooks down dark alleys, driving fast, rescuing damsels, kicking in doors and justice like it was in the cartoons on Saturday mornings.

A couple of my mates at the 1st Commando Regiment decided to start a humanitarian aid organisation called Australian Aid International. My mate Frank told me his plans and asked me if I would consider helping. By this stage I had done a complex and expansive special forces medic's course in the army, and had a bit of experience in treating casualties here and there. I liked the idea of what Frank was saying. AAI was going to be a fast, efficient agency formed to respond to disasters around the world in places where other

aid organisations were unable to go because of climatic conditions, remote locations or danger. It ticked all the right boxes
for me, and still does. It still operates that way, and hopefully
always will. So I said yes to Frank, thinking that a year or two
later I would end up going to Africa or somewhere to help AAI
for a couple of weeks. Nope.

About a week later the Central Asian Earthquake occurred
in Pakistan and 86 000 people were killed. I took leave from
work and got over there as soon as I could. I was pretty much
hooked straightaway. Until that time I didn't know a thing
about the humanitarian sector, but what I saw excited and
amazed me. This sort of work seemed to satisfy the part of
me that wanted to be involved in the world's big picture, the
part that wanted to be involved in a large, organised agency
that worked as a team, and it was a practical way to apply
my ideals of social justice. Perfect. AAI has seen me work in
Pakistan, numerous times in Thailand and on the frantic and
precarious Thai/Burma border, Myanmar, and repeatedly in
Timor-Leste and Indonesia. I am still a program manager for
AAI, and hope I can remain in this role.

Jim, a good friend of mine, told me years ago that we were
men waiting. Neither of us knew what for. We had filled our
heads with the training and experience to handle any situation;
we just didn't have the forum to apply what we knew. After the
Pakistan earthquake in 2005, we knew. It feels good to know.

I was not sure I could be a family man, policeman, soldier
and humanitarian all at the same time. A number of other
significant players held a similar view. In 2006 I decided to
seek employment as a contracted security consultant. I wasn't

dissatisfied with the police, but when I looked at my superiors, who were all great guys doing a really hard task, I just didn't want their job. If I didn't want to be promoted into those positions, I shouldn't really stay. I left the police on good terms, and have a great deal of respect for the many people I know who are still police and for Victoria Police as an organisation. The world was, and is, insecure; I had developed a highly ethical and moral way of applying and achieving security, and I can really see where the humanitarian and security sectors share a lot of common ground. I knew I had skills that I could apply to both. Becoming a security consultant was going to augment working for AAI very well.

I worked in Iraq for all of 2007, first as a police instructor for the Iraqi National Police then as a contracted private security detachment member. All the nightmares about working in Iraq are true in some way. Our friends were killed, we were shelled and shot at, and we observed the community in that country tearing itself apart. A private security detachment member is like a soldier who provides security to some group of people or important infrastructure. We usually provided security for the road transport that was our shuttle of staff back and forth from Baghdad to the police academy where we worked. The conflict in Iraq has seen this industry rise exponentially, and it is an imperfect solution to the need for security personnel where soldiers are unavailable to do the job.

If I get a chance to explain my work in Iraq, no one considers me, or anyone I worked with, a mercenary. Though, in purely technical terms, we were all selling our military skills to a non-state entity. That is the very definition of a mercenary.

The word mercenary conjures up images of guns for hire doing dirty work and ultimately killing for a commercial reason. That's not me at all. I moved into that role because I wanted to make sure that our staff were secure, and that we made good ethical decisions about providing security. I can promise you that every time we rolled out of our gates we considered the safety of our passengers, our own safety and the safety of the public in Iraq. I know that had our positions been reversed, and I was a disadvantaged man struggling for survival in my occupied country, then I would be likely to use my skills for violence against those rich jailers who drove their armoured vehicles through my neighbourhood. You might be surprised that I never got any arguments when I talked to the rest of the team about that.

I have finished that role for now, but would go back to it given the right circumstances. This seems strange to many people. This is not some quest for more adventure, or violence – far from it. Knowing there is a moral grounding for the work and reasonably safe conditions would help, but feeling that I can also provide a humanitarian edge to security operations would be very rewarding to me. We will see.

I worked in those jobs listed above and a number of others as well. I always looked for something that would pay the bills, but that taught me something too. I like activities and sports that can get me into trouble. I like surfing, diving, mountain bike riding and sea kayaking. Tennis, croquet and spectator sports never really did it for me. There's nothing wrong with them, but they just don't blow my hair back.

Alright. That's me, but where am I going with this book?

I started thinking about writing the book because I had so many good stories from unusual situations I have been involved in. But really, every time I wanted to write it, I thought it was a bit hollow, so I didn't bother. To me it was just some guy sounding off about how interesting he thought he was.

One night I spoke to a mate of mine, who I hadn't seen in years, and he asked me to recount some of the good and bad moments from the last few years. I did and we laughed through some good stories and just about cried because of some others. Towards the end of the night he stumped me.

'So what?' he said. 'What have you got to pass on? What did you learn that you can tell somebody?'

He was right. Who cares what happened? What is important is whether it was an entertaining story and how it can instruct us on life. At the time I gave him some weak answer, but on the way home I thought about it properly. I decided to take every story I had recounted, and look at why I remembered it, and why I retell that particular story. I remember stories that are funny, that make me laugh even thinking about them. But usually, I tell stories because there is a moral or some voice of advice in there somewhere, among the humour.

Great. That made writing this book a good deal easier. I looked at the stories I had, and grouped them into categories of why a person may want to hear it or why I might want to tell it. Subjects jumped out at me. Pay attention to your surroundings. Emotions like fear and how they affect our lives. Having a sense of humour, and why that is important. That's what we have here now.

I have something else I had better say. You could read this

book and think that I'm some sort of angel, always doing the right thing, helping people constantly, and getting through the tough parts miraculously unscathed. Not true. I have made all the mistakes that anybody else has, and done all the bad things you have, and probably a few more that you didn't know existed. That's not what this book is about, and there is probably little real value in those stories. I have not shied away from them because I want to appear like some knight on a white charger, they're just not that funny, or instructive enough. Besides, medics in the army have a saying, 'We bury our mistakes'.

Now that you have read this far, you can jump to any point in the book and start at that chapter, with no need to read the book chronologically. It is not arranged that way at all. Knowing what you now know, you can read Chapter 7 first. It's a cracker. Still, starting at the front is something to do for lack of a plan.

Please enjoy.

CHAPTER 1

Captive to experience

8 out of 10 people who own samurai swords are wankers

I'm going to have to start this book by apologising. I know there are people reading this chapter title right now saying, 'Yeah, but he's not talking about me.' Well, I'm sorry, but, in my opinion, if you own a samurai sword, there is a better than good chance that you are, unfortunately, a wanker.

I have not just invented this; unfortunately, I have come to believe this through bitter experience. We are all captive to our experiences and when it comes to people who own samurai swords, mine are all bad. As a general duties police officer you are called to all manner of incidents that occur in shops, factories, hotels, public facilities, hospitals, you name it. If something goes really wrong in our lives, we call the police, and, by and large, the police respond, either by talking on the phone or by physically attending. Often, before anyone else can go and try to fix the problem, the general duties police officer must first go and check it out. We seem to call the police for everything nowadays, not just crime. Neighbour's dog is barking—call the police. Somebody stole your parking spot yesterday—call the police. Noisy party down the street—call the police. Cat is stuck somewhere—call the police. Car is parked across the road and you haven't seen it in the area before—call the police. Had an argument with your sister— call the police. In many households people have forgotten that, as members of society, we are allowed to have animated arguments with family members without registering said argument with a state or federally administered agency.

Strangely, this sort of thing did not frustrate me the way it did some of my colleagues, and you become very good at dealing with people—smart people, not so smart people, good people and bad people, the insane and charming and down-right rude and obnoxious. I enjoyed walking into a situation, looking around, speaking for a minute or two, watching how people interact with each other, and then making my assess-ment. My assessment was never about who was right and who was wrong, because in domestic arguments that was never clear. My assessment just gave me an idea of the things I had to say. Some people needed to be agreed with. Some people needed to be argued against. Some people wanted to feel righ-teous, and some people just needed us to listen to their side of the story, nothing else, just listen. The idea was to leave the house, hotel, park, hospital, apartment or whatever not having to return, and without anyone handcuffed. You might not think this is true, but for police officers, that's the best possible result.

But, back to my reason for the samurai sword = wanker statement. Responding to all these incidents necessitates you entering people's homes (and usually they aren't expecting guests), and I can tell you, very often when I went to the house of a person who was causing some sort of trouble—someone who was violent or about to be arrested on a warrant, or was difficult, obnoxious, drunk and yelling at the neighbours, or otherwise a knob—there was a samurai sword present, either hanging on the wall in the hallway or in the lounge or bedroom. In the case of criminals, or people who, for some reason, live in perpetual fear of attack and therefore require the use of a sword at a moment's notice, the sword would be left leaning against the wall, inside the door, or, alternatively, next to the bed. Wankers all.

I will illustrate my hypothesis (can I call this a hypothesis?) with examples. One day I was working in the western suburbs of Melbourne with Vince, a really cool policeman. I always enjoyed working with Vince because he was steady and courageous (not all police are particularly courageous) and he didn't make stupid ego-based decisions (some do make stupid ego-based decisions). Vince was very direct and was willing to put himself at risk for the job. Also, and more importantly, he was good fun to be around.

Ok, so Vince and I respond to an incident where an adult male has been drinking all morning, has thrown his girlfriend out of their house, smashed the house up and threatened violence on anybody who approached the house. Uncool. The girlfriend has also contacted the psych services that have been treating him for depression. (We will talk about mental illness and police interaction with the mentally ill many times before you have finished this book.)

When we get to the house the girlfriend is crying and looks like he has been bashing her about, but she will not say that. She says he was not directly violent to her, but needs the police because she's really worried he will either hurt himself or the psych doctors when they turn up. She's waiting just down the street from the house, so we ask her for all the information we need to make an assessment of the situation before we go into the house to talk to this guy. She's definitely scared, not just putting on a turn for the police, and she tells us that he has been thinking about suicide lately, though he hasn't actually said he will kill himself today. He's an ex-army guy, so, having some army experience myself, I propose to just go in and try to talk to him, guy to guy, soldier to soldier, whatever will appeal. Remember, the best result for us is if we speak calmly and leave in a few minutes with nobody in handcuffs or hurt.

The girlfriend gives me the keys to the house and tells me he has a number of samurai swords inside. Bingo. Wanker. Of course, I had already pegged this guy as a wanker anyway, for hitting his girlfriend. Oh, and naturally he hasn't got one sword, he has a number of them. He must be quite the connoisseur. Well, at this point many police will pull back, call in a police tactical team, get a supervisor, air support and extra police to set up a cordon, get an ambulance and fire brigade on standby, and then go home because the shift has ended.

Now, I am not brave, and I will repeat this many times in this book, but that response is just ridiculous. I will at least go and have a talk to the bloke and see how he is. I would prefer to open the door, go in and say hello and see if we can get to the bottom of this without involving every other police resource in the state of Victoria. I don't think I'm wrong in that approach. I'm hoping to appeal to him by talking about the army, finding some common ground, appearing as friendly and nonconfrontational as possible. If he comes at me with a sword I will run away. No problem. Also, and this is a big also, I have a gun. In any computer game or Hollywood film you have ever seen, guns beat swords. Every time. If they didn't, I suppose I would have carried a sword all those years, instead of a .38 Special.

Anyway, Vince goes around the back and I go to the front door, call the guy's name and announce myself. No response, but fair enough as there is REALLY loud thrash music playing. I look in the large lounge-room window and see that the guy is sitting on a couch facing away from me, leaning forward, with his head in his hands. He doesn't exactly look like he's ready to repel any advance we might make into his house, and seems calm. I give Vince about 30 seconds to get around the back and then put the key in the front door. Vince comes up on the radio to tell me he has entered the back door and is in the kitchen.

Then the girlfriend runs up and says, 'He used to have an old pistol in the house. I don't think he has it anymore. I haven't seen it in a long time. I don't even know if it works. Sorry, I should have told you before.' Ahh, yeah, you should have. Well, Vince is inside now and I'm concerned that he will confront the guy any second. I tell Vince what's going on via the radio.

I open the door and walk right up behind the guy. He's totally oblivious. In a situation like this we always have a good look around the general area to see if there is anything close by that could be utilised as a weapon. Well, yeah, the two unsheathed samurai swords sitting on the couch next to him could count as weapons. I can't see anything else around that's more dangerous than the swords, but I can't see everything on the low table in front of him. I'm more than slightly concerned about the situation as Vince pops his head around the corner from the kitchen. The guy has not seen him because he still has his head in his hands. I draw my revolver and aim it squarely at the back of the guy's head. Vince can see what I'm doing and has obviously cottoned on to the situation. We don't usually pull guns out just as a conversation starter, although that ALWAYS does start a conversation.

A few seconds pass as Vince weighs up the situation. I quickly change the game plan because I believe it is better for me just to shut up and stay behind the guy and be ready to trump any move he might make. Really, I have a gun pointed to the back of his head, so, ultimately, only one person is going to get hurt if he tries anything.

Vince announces his presence and the guy makes a move. People say it over and over, but it really is amazing, in critical situations, how much time you seem to have to think through the circumstances and analyse the situation. The guy doesn't go for one of the two swords sitting either side of him. Now, this gets me thinking. He must have something he thinks is better than the swords. The wheels turn in my head and I come up with ... gun.

He's reaching forward to the coffee table in front of him and there, mostly covered by a newspaper, is the handgrip of a pistol. I race forward, hit him in the back of the head with my revolver and yell, 'Don't you fucking dare or I'll blow your head off!'

Well, it does the trick. He knows I have the drop on him

and he leans back. I assume he correctly assessed the heavy metal object that impacted the back of his head was my gun. I grab the two swords and throw them behind me. Vince comes forward and grabs the gun. It's an imitation Browning pistol. Wanker. He was just about killed going for a fake pistol.

The guy was actually quite calm immediately after this and we didn't even handcuff him. He was alright, really, and the correct action in this situation was exactly what we did, which was to get him psychiatric care.

Despite the fact that he had been seconds away from a shoot-out with police that he was definitely undergunned for, and that I had belted him in the back of the head and threatened to kill him, we were all instant mates. Vince and I didn't feel any angst towards this guy, he was clearly mentally ill, and he was quite happy with the way we treated him. In fact, when the psych services arrived and started to talk to him, he was very complimentary about us and obviously hostile to them. Hmmm, maybe he had a clear picture about some things…

That is not the only samurai sword = wanker story that led me to develop my hypothesis. On another occasion I was called to assist some other police officers with the arrest of a suspect and processing of a hydroponic marijuana crop. It would stun you to know how many of these things are out there in the suburbs of capital cities around Australia. It is big business, relatively easy money for the criminals involved, and society (through the courts) has tended to take a pretty relaxed view about it. The fact remains, it is largely organised by criminal gangs that are into all manner of crimes, and they use the profits and infrastructure associated with these networks to organise much more serious crimes.

My job on this day is to be there to control the arrested suspect. I walk in after the other police have arrested this guy. He's about 6 feet tall, medium build and probably around 30 years old. Everything has gone very smoothly, and he's in handcuffs. As I walk in through the front entrance hallway of the nice middle-class house, I see the Wanker's Pennant hanging from the wall: a full size samurai sword. Great. However, the guy is calm and cooperating, so I am too. I'm polite and relaxed with the guy. It's easier for everyone if police treat suspects in a civil manner. There is nothing to be gained by the police acting all high and mighty in this situation. We are already walking around his house, poking about as we please, looking through his personal belongings, while he is sorrowful, in handcuffs, thinking about the turn his life has just taken. No need to gloat. Also, very soon police have to conduct a formal interview with him, and there's no need to get him all hot under the collar before that process, which can take a long time. It can also take two hours or so just to remove the hydroponics equipment and associated evidence from the house.

By this time, his parents have arrived and are very perplexed. They legally own the house but don't live there, so they're not responsible for the marijuana crop. However, at the end of the day, I believe they would have known what was happening, as they lived just around the corner and even a cursory look around the inside of the house told you what was going on.

After about half an hour of sitting in a relaxed position on a couch, the suspect decides he wants to leave as he believes this situation is causing him and his mother way too much stress and anxiety. He says, 'That's enough now, I'm leaving and you have to let me go outside. I know my rights and you can't keep me here.'

To which I naturally reply, 'Yep, sure mate. Just bend over a bit so I can undo those pesky handcuffs and you're free to go.'

He doesn't get the joke and bends over.

'Mate, you're under arrest. You're not going anywhere. Just relax, it won't be long before we get this thing over with.'

He's not having it and tries to stand up. I put my hand firmly on his shoulder and push him back down. Not happening. He realises that he's not going to win the stand-up-while-a-large-policeman-pushes-you-down competition and sits down for a minute, but is obviously agitated. I leave my hand on his shoulder, pressing firmly.

'Seeing me here like this is causing my mother great stress. I am going.'

Then he says it. 'If this causes my mother stress I'm going to take that sword off the wall and cut you up, you fucking blah, blah, blah...'

His tirade goes on for about a minute, and frankly I tune out as I couldn't really care what this guy says to me. As you can imagine, it's pretty rare that somebody comes up with a new insult for a police officer. There is certainly nothing new in what this guy is saying. However, threatening me, while handcuffed and in my care, is ridiculous. Also, I don't like it.

Clearly, this causes his mother more distress than anything

that has happened to that point.

Yeah, right. I smile and lean down to whisper in his ear.

'Your mother can leave anytime she likes. You and I are staying here, then I am personally taking you to the police cells. If you threaten to kill me again, I'll make you wish you hadn't.'

I have a gleam in my eye when he looks up at me. There is always quite a bit of theatre in how I interact with people in these matters. Making people believe you're some sort of unhinged, sadistic psychopath is much easier and safer than actually being one. He looks at me and shuts up. He's probably thinking about the long night he has ahead of him, in police cells, with me to look after him.

A few minutes later he tries a new tactic. Well, it's new to him, but police officers see it all the time. He starts getting the shakes then goes into a sort of seizure, or at least what he thinks going into a seizure looks like. He is totally uncommunicative, frothing at the mouth and writhing around on the ground making guttural noises. I don't do a thing. I don't even acknowledge it as he bounces around the floor, thrashing his legs about. A couple of the other police officers who are present look at me, wondering if I'm going to take some action to assist him. Instead, I sort of look away as if I'm suddenly really interested in the crappy art hanging from the walls in the house.

After about 30 seconds of maximum effort he's exhausted. I still have hardly even looked in his direction. He suddenly stops in a weird position with his hands still secured behind his back and says, 'Aren't you going to do anything?'

I smile. 'Nope. But I'm glad you're better now.'

Wanker.

STANLEY KNIFE

That story, and a number of others just like it, where the common thread was a wanker owning a samurai sword, was exactly why I came up with this hypothesis.

So yeah, I admit that I don't actually have any statistics, but you'll have to take it from me that most people who have samurai swords are wankers. I have guessed about 8 out of 10. I was going to say 9 out of 10 but thought that was a bit extreme, really. There must be legitimate samurai sword owners. Though, I must admit it took me a while to think of a legitimate reason to have a sword kicking around the house. I mean, you don't use them to cut up the carrots for the evening meal or for pruning in the garden. A Stanley knife is generally more useful for most odd jobs around the house.

Sure, if I think about it hard, there are reasons why you might own a samurai sword. So, I thought I would attempt to categorise all samurai sword owners into neat groups. We'll see how it goes. If you're reading this and aren't sure which group you're in, I implore you, don't try to categorise yourself, but ask somebody for his or her honest, objective opinion. Of course you will.

FIRST GROUP

I will start at the most legitimate end of the scale, and head down from there. First, there are people who are Japanese. I reckon if you're Japanese but living anywhere outside of Japan, you can automatically have a samurai sword. You could still be a wanker, but I reckon you have a sort of birthright allowing you to own a samurai sword. In fact, there should be more of it. I'm all for it. It's like an American having a cowboy hat, a Frenchman having a striped shirt, or a Russian having a bottle of vodka. No arguments here.

SECOND GROUP

In this group I'm going to throw in anyone who has been presented a samurai sword as a gift. I don't mean from your mate who got it from Cash Converters, I mean from a Japanese person, to show their esteem for some service you have rendered. I put that in because I have a large wooden hunting bow and a set of arrows that were given to me by a former resistance commander from the civil war in Bougainville, Papua New Guinea, while I served there with the Australian Army. I reckon that could happen with a samurai sword too, and you should be proud of ownership under those circumstances.

THIRD GROUP

Next is any person who either got the sword while fighting the Japanese in World War II (or any other time) or has had it passed down from someone who got it under those circumstances. No arguments here—legitimate ownership as far as I'm concerned.

FOURTH GROUP

The fourth, but second last group, would be legitimate collectors who research the art of making the swords, their history, the metallurgy involved, and have a genuine cultural or scientific interest. I appreciate that originally produced samurai swords are an amazing piece of craftsmanship. You could be OK if you're in this group. However, persons who consider themselves to be in this group do not get an automatic wanker pass. If you're in this group, but have ever photographed or videoed yourself slashing away against some unseen foe as if you were a feudal warrior/ninja turtle, then you're out. Or, if on inspection of your home, there are any chop marks on trees or on the doorframe of the garage, then you're gone. Wanker. Sorry, relegation to GROUP FIVE.

The groups I have already mentioned constitute about 20 per cent of samurai sword owners.

FIFTH GROUP

That leaves our last group. This is the group that I reckon 80 per cent of samurai sword owners belong in. They bought them from markets, weirdos, mates, shops, wherever. These people think they're cool and tough at the same time by being samurai sword owners, and have generally brandished them at some point in their lives while drunk at parties, or at the neighbour's dog or bloke up the street. The people in this group are wankers without mitigation of the circumstances in any way, I'm afraid.

I realise that there will be some disappointed and probably offended people reading this. I'm sorry, and you may want me to start a new category for 'I saw it cheap at the local trash-and-treasure market and thought it would look good'. Or, 'I have it to keep fit by training swordsmanship with'. Again, sorry, not going to happen. Also, I have never been into a house where the existing décor really said to me, 'This room would look great with a samurai sword on the wall'. Please feel entirely free to ask any interior decorator you can find, but I don't like your chances.

Remember, mathematically:

$\frac{8}{10} \times z$ = wanker, where z equals samurai sword

Remember to get somebody else to decide in which group you belong. Good luck.

According to the 2006 census, conducted by the Australian Bureau of Statistics, there are 40 968 persons in Australia who identify themselves as Japanese. Potential legitimate owners, every single one.

CHAPTER 2

Mental illness

'Mentally ill people are just like you and I, you know? Only, well, crazy.'

Police officers in modern democracies deal with the full range of difficult and sensitive issues that face our societies. People think of police officers dealing with crime only. That is not true. In fact, actual crime probably accounts for about 50 per cent of the incidents the police respond to.

You know I have had a lot of jobs, but being a police officer was definitely the one that required me to have the most information close at hand, in fact, committed to memory: state and federal legislation, local laws, traffic and criminal law and these laws are changing all the time. You also need to retain a huge amount of intelligence about who does what in your neighbourhood, which criminals are active, how they usually commit their crimes and how to catch them. These were the factors that made it a hard job, but also very enjoyable.

All police officers have their pet hates. Categories of jobs they just don't like responding to, or situations they find awkward or uncomfortable. Tough luck, you still have to go and do them. It might be to attend to traffic accidents or domestic disputes. Everyone has tasks, which are, let's say, their least favourite.

EXTREMELY DEPRESSED

Police very often deal with members of the public with mental health issues. I mean VERY often. Some weeks that seems like all you do. These people are generally not criminals per se, even if their actions cause them to commit crimes, so they have to be treated in a manner that befits this status. This can be a real juggling act, especially when they are violent.

I remember taking one of our regular customers to a psych facility in Melbourne's west, where he was very well known. We will call him Kevin. Unfortunately, he was known for his violence and bad temper and on this occasion had been really tearing up the house where he lived with his girlfriend. I was working with a friend of mine, David, who was a great police-man. He had a calm, easy style when talking to the public, and was very patient, a trait that not all police officers could claim. Our client's girlfriend had called the police because, in the course of busting up the house, Kevin had told her he was going to kill himself. That means we have to transport him to a psych facility where they will look after him. Really, the only reason the police have to arrest a person in these circumstances is when they pose a threat to somebody else, or themselves. When it comes to a threat to themselves, the police officers have to believe that the person is really capable and ready to attempt to kill himself or herself. There is a gap in legislative power here. When a police officer is presented with a person who is extremely depressed but does not actually say that they want to kill themselves, there is little they can do. If you contact the relevant authority, it is my experience that they might get back to you in two or three days. I don't think it's responsible to leave a person in this condition alone for a few days. So I admit that I would routinely arrest a person in these circumstances and transport them to a psych hospital. When I got to the hospital, I would tell the staff that the patient said they were going to kill themselves. Not a perfect system, but probably the right thing to do.

It was always a bit of a guessing game with Kevin as to how he would behave. He was a gun nut so he always liked to talk about our police service pistols and going shooting or hunting or whatever. In that way, it was always easy to start a conversation with him. I had arrested Kevin twice in the three months prior to this incident, and once he wanted to fight the whole way and the other time he was a perfect gentleman. Every time you deal with somebody, you deal with ALL the issues they have had with police since they were born. Did the police treat them badly? Did they see the police as helping them out of the terrible time they were having? Sometimes the police are the very root of their fears or paranoia. I have met many people, in an excited psychotic state, who were convinced I was there to kill them. Even the most congenial bloke you know would find it difficult to strike up a reasonable conversation in those circumstances. It was always hard to tell what you would be presented with. I was aware that Kevin had been arrested at least three other times recently, so he was earning Frequent (Police) Traveller miles quite well.

When we arrived at the house our guy was outside and we spoke to him calmly. I had a good look at him and tried to get a feel for how he would act. He was a bit drunk and covered in mud, seemingly from dirt in the front yard. It didn't look like he had just gotten dirty in the course of doing something.

It looked like he had deliberately covered himself in mud. I stood a bit closer and had a discreet sniff. No worries, it was mud, I think, or I hoped. He was wearing a pair of blue jeans cut into shorts and nothing on top, despite the fact that it was about 7.30 at night and about 12 degrees Celsius. He was calm and easy to talk to. We were looking good.

It was shaping up to be a pretty easy job, all things considered. Kevin was relaxed and speaking to us about his problems and even suggested himself that he needed to go to hospital. In this situation, that is music to your ears, believe me. Not surprisingly, many people don't want to go anywhere near a psych hospital, no matter how nice and friendly everyone there is. I wouldn't, I can tell you that. OK. So far so good. Kevin was being very gentlemanly. No handcuffs, no worries. Excellent, job well done David and Nathan.

Just as I was about to get him to step into the back of the divisional van Kevin changed his mind. Apparently he wasn't having it. He stood up straight, made a fist and took a swing at me. It flew past me as I stepped back. If a criminal had tried that move he would have been laying on the ground now, with a sore, well, everything, and seeing stars like in the cartoons. But this wasn't the same at all. We looked at each other wondering what was going to happen next. I looked into his eyes and did not read any more violence directed at me, or did I? I reckoned he would respond to a good speaking to, so I decided to yell at him.

'Turn around and put your hands behind your back, right now!'

Really, he was only a little guy, and I think he was quite

stunned that I didn't cave his head in. He looked at me with a shocked expression on his face, and did exactly what I asked.

'Sorry about that, Mr Mullins.'

He must have been 6 inches shorter than me, and he was giving away about 40 kilos in weight if he wanted to fight. He would want to be able to punch above his weight if he was going to have a proper shot. I decided that we did need handcuffs now. The time for a nice drive to hospital without handcuffs had expired.

Well, we were friends again. Wasn't that nice? Then, as I was about to put the handcuffs on, he had second thoughts – well, I suppose by this stage they were third thoughts. Again he struggled to get free and looked like he was ready to plant one on me. He cocked his arm back ready to throw a punch. I couldn't tell whether he had lured me in by acting calm for a second or if he just couldn't make up his mind. Either way, I was a lot closer to him this time, and simply grabbed him around the upper body, lifted him up off the ground and threw him down on the road. Hard. His crash with the tarmac was not softened or mitigated in any way by him getting a hand or foot down to break his fall. It would've hurt anyone, but a guy like this—unfit, half drunk, nearly naked, and whose main source of nutrition, for the past three years, had been supplied by Fosters and Benson and Hedges? He was out for the count.

Police are in a different position to the rest of society. This is not a fight in a bar or on a football field. It cannot be a matter of trading blows on equal terms, according to the Marquess of Queensberry Rules. I have to win, and he has to lose, that's it. If somebody tries to punch me on the street, I will walk away, no problems. I couldn't care less and I don't need to win. As a police officer, you cannot walk away from physical confrontation. Police decide who is under arrest and who isn't. You don't undecide because the person you are trying to arrest suddenly isn't playing along. Also, I should say here that it's safer for everyone concerned when you deal with somebody once they are on the ground. If you think about the alternatives they are clear. I could have hit him so many times in the face that I rendered him unconscious, I could have hit him with a baton and knocked him out, or I could have shot him dead or sprayed him with capsicum spray. With a millisecond to react I did what was safest for him and for me. I picked him up and threw him down.

I smiled and put the handcuffs on him while he stared at me in abject horror. He was gasping for breath, not able to talk at all and unable to resist any more than a teddy bear could. He was totally shocked by the events and clearly needed a moment. He looked like a puppet whose strings had all suddenly been cut.

I said, 'Mate, that was silly. Totally unnecessary.'

I lifted him into the back of the van and drove to the hospital. Halfway there he obviously started to feel better and was screaming for us to stop. Fair enough. I stopped the van on the side of the freeway and got out to have a talk. As I opened the back of the van I could see that he actually was sick. He looked terrible and, as soon as the door swung open, he vomited all over himself and started sobbing. I bet he was feeling pretty miserable right now. Imagine feeling that bad, stuck in a police van, handcuffed, nearly naked, sick as a dog and covered in mud and your own vomit, which you can't wipe off because your hands are secured behind your back. He didn't even look up.

'Can you take me to hospital please, sir?'

'Yeah mate. That's where we're going. Just hold tight.'

When we got to the hospital the psych nurses looked at Kevin and were disgusted. I told them exactly what happened. They were pretty good about it. I might have thought about toning down my description of throwing him on the ground when speaking to some people but it wasn't necessary in this case. These psych nurses were a pretty hardened bunch who, in my experience, did a remarkable job in dealing with these situations. One of them grabbed me by the arm and leant in for a quiet word.

'He has to have a shower before he comes in.'

The psych nurse gestured to an outdoor showerhead protruding from the ceiling to the left of the entrance. It didn't look too good, and I knew that Kevin would freeze in the open air. Even I thought this was a bit much, and this bloke had tried to attack me twice in the last twenty minutes. So I gave it a try.

'Come on. Can't he have one inside? He's freezing.'

'Nope, he's not coming in here like that.'

Personally, I think that was a mistake, and a terrible way to treat this guy. I knew that he would lock this scene into his mind as if it was the part in *First Blood* where Rambo gets hosed down at the police station. (I was pretty sure Kevin would have seen *Rambo* at least twenty times.) Also, he would relate it to the police experience, feeling that the police were the instrument of his outdoor shower. I felt like walking away and letting the hospital security staff do the job, but couldn't. Technically, he was very much in my care, and until properly admitted to hospital, would remain so.

I held him under the shower and turned the water on. I got totally soaked too, but the sounds he made were pathetic. Fair enough. I reckoned this was not the best Friday night he had ever had. Not even close.

I gave him a quick wash and pushed past the nurse into the foyer area. He was still dirty but having him out in the cold any longer would have been ridiculous.

'Well, he's in now.'

There was no arguing with that.

I was holding Kevin by the arm when a psych doctor came up to me, looked at him, looked at me and shook his head. He probably thought I had bashed this bloke, covered him in vomit and mud, induced his sickness and then decided to do some sort of weird water torture to him. I will never forget it. The doctor cocked his head, fixed a disgusted look on his face and I knew he was going to say something that he thought was vitally important. It was like he was a Shakespearian stage actor and needed to affect a dramatic look for the delivery of the coming stanza. He was a professional psychiatrist, he probably went to school for ten years to learn his trade, so I was actually really intrigued to hear what he was going to say to me, though I had already guessed that I wasn't going to like it.

'Mentally ill people are just like you and I, you know? Only, well, crazy.'

He immediately turned around and walked away. Astounding. He could not have dumbfounded me any more fully if he had said, 'Senior Constable Mullins, I'm in love with you and I want us to fly away together.'

For a second I couldn't tell whether he was serious, mentally ill himself, or an extremely good practical joker. Nope. He was serious. I don't think I'm a particularly sensitive type, but I knew he was supposed to be. He made this statement right in front of Kevin. As well as being highly insensitive, his statement made no sense at all and added nothing to help the situation, other than pissing me off. I left the hospital shaking my head. I looked at it as being akin to him saying, 'Handicapped people are just like you and I, you know? Only, well, retards.'

Yeah right, Kevin's mental health was in good hands with that doctor. I walked away thinking, 'I suppose I'll see you again soon, Kevin.'

Not all mentally ill persons the police deal with are violent, or causing any inconvenience to anyone but themselves. Some people cause a bit of trouble to their neighbours and are a minor annoyance but are, in actuality, harmless. However, if you don't have experience with or don't understand their behaviour, these interactions can be very disconcerting.

I remember one night, not long after I had joined the police, that illustrates this point perfectly. I was at a police station in Melbourne's western suburbs. Constable Mullins manning the phones on Saturday night. All sorts of complaints, enquiries and pleas for help get directed through a police station's phones. Everything you can think of gets rung in. On a Saturday night it seems to be everything you can think of, and a hundred other things you didn't think of.

At about 10 PM a lady phones in. She's in a frantic state. The tone of her voice immediately commands my attention.

'Please help, there's an insane man out the front of my house.'

I take her name, date of birth and address straightaway, and turn around to the senior constable in the room and start to give him the details: who/what/where. This is so, if need be, he can immediately get on the radio and start to direct a police unit to the address. The woman is about 40 years old and home alone.

Chris is what they refer to as a bushy-tailed Senior Connie. This means he has been around since they were riding horses to jobs and has seen and done it all. It also means he should be a senior sergeant but isn't because he doesn't tow the line or is happier at the lower ranks. Experienced, but not dynamic, you might say.

Chris leans back and considers the details we have so far. He tells me to get the whole picture before we do anything. Fair enough. I ask the woman exactly what is happening.

'Well, I can see him through my window right now. He's creeping around the garden and hiding in the bushes. I don't think he can see me, though.'

'OK. How long has he been there?'

'Oh, about ten minutes this time, but he has done this before. Look, my doors and windows are locked but please hurry.'

She sounds really scared.

'What happened the last time he did this?'

'Well, you guys came and scared him away, thank God.

Look, I really need you to get here now. He's obsessed with me and won't stop. This has been going on for too long.'

I'm starting to get worried now that we don't have any police units on the way there and turn around and give a look to Chris. Sure, it's a busy Saturday night in the peak summer period, but I think this requires immediate action.

He gives me the 'keep talking' sign language, so I do. I'm also interested to find out if she knows any more about the man in the front yard who is obsessed with her. If she does know him we can start doing ID checks on the computer, find out who he is and what information there is about him. This way we can assess exactly what threat this guy poses to her/us.

'How do you know it's the same man, and how do you know him?'

'Well, I suppose I don't really know him very well, but he has always wanted a relationship with me. He's infatuated with me and it has to stop.'

Bingo, she will know exactly the information I need to ID the guy.

'OK. What's his name?'

'His surname is Smith. His first name is Robert.'

I'm writing down the information with my free hand. I type Smith, Robert into our identity database, but as you could guess, it's a pretty common name so I need an age or address to narrow it down.

'Do you know his date of birth or even roughly how old he is?'

'Well, I don't know his date of birth but he's about my age.'

'OK, how do you know him?' As I speak I'm looking down

the list of Robert Smiths to see if any are in the correct age bracket.

'Well, I don't really. I went to a concert years ago and he was there and since then he has been totally infatuated with me.'

'OK, what's his address?'

'Oh, I don't know. I think he lives in England.'

Pause. Pause. Thinking. Thinking. Hmmm.

'Ahh, is he a singer?'

'Yes, that's right.'

'Ahh, are you talking about Robert Smith, the lead singer of The Cure?' I felt stupid saying it, but had to do it.

I turn around and look at Chris. He has a very satisfied smirk on his face. No wonder he wanted to keep me talking to her. He obviously knew what was going on. My attitude changes a bit.

'Are the rest of the band there?'

'They'll be around somewhere. They always are.'

'OK. Look, The Cure is one of my favourite bands so I'll see what I can do. Are there any other people who are infatuated with you that we should know about?'

'Yes. The band Wire is also infatuated with me.'

'OK. Um, we won't be coming around. I'm sure you're OK so don't worry about The Cure. Don't worry about Wire either, while I think of it. Do you have a doctor that normally treats you for any form of illness?'

So it goes on for the next few minutes with me trying to explain that she should speak to her treating doctor and tell them how she feels and what has been going on.

When I get off the phone Chris tells me that she rings once

or twice a month and it only seems to happen Saturday night when she has had a few drinks. He had known exactly what she was going to say as soon as I gave him her name, but wanted to see what would happen.

A year or so later I found out that she was a pillar in the community, never drank in public, or other than Saturday nights, carried out a great deal of charity work and was always ready to help people in her little neighbourhood. I think we can totally forgive her quirk about The Cure.

Dealing with people who are mentally ill is all about relationships. You're need to establish your bona fides with them, to prove that you there to help. That is easier said than done, though.

One day I got called to a set of ground floor units, about six in all, in which about ten mentally ill people lived. The particular lady we had to see had apparently barricaded herself in and was scared of aliens abducting her. She had not left the flat in days. One of her relatives had called and wanted us to check on her welfare. I was working with a big guy, Silas. He was nice man and good policeman, but didn't really have a sense of humour about dealing with the mentally ill.

We get to the doorway and call the woman. She won't really explain anything through the door and won't remove the barricade. Silas will. He's had enough and forces the door open. She is not too upset and calms down when I tell her that the aliens won't come while we are there, and she can put the barricade back when we leave. You don't want to agree with their paranoia, but it's pretty hard to argue with a mentally ill person that aliens do not exist. It would be hard enough to argue that with most people. So, you basically don't try.

The house stinks. I mean the house stinks. I have been in plenty of smelly places but this is absolutely putrid. We ask her but she doesn't know what the smell is and I'm not that keen to investigate it either. I'm pretty happy to leave that be.

She's OK. I encourage her to talk to her doctor and make a note to contact the agency that treats the residents in this place. But there's a catch.

She says, 'How do I get in touch with you if I need help with the aliens or whatever?'

I look at Silas and he's not making a move. He's like a statue. He hasn't said one word to her since caving in her barricade and coming into the room. He's obviously not enjoying the crazy lady antics or stench. It's hard to blame him.

'OK. Give me a piece of paper and I'll write down my contact information.'

Silas looks at me in disgust, but we really can't just leave her there and not attempt to help her in some way.

We walk out to the car and Silas breaks his silence as we're about to jump in.

'Mate, you never give a person like that your contact details. She'll annoy you for months.'

'I didn't. I gave her yours.'

Every experience I had dealing with mentally ill people taught me that there was a lot I didn't know. It was hard at times, because no matter how smooth a talker you were, or how theatrical you could get, often negotiation just didn't work.

In the case of an ordinary person, given some time, I'm sure I can convince them that they don't want to fight me, that I'm not a bad bloke, that I'll treat them fairly. In this way, it was extremely rare for me to get into physical confrontations with people. The fact that I was a 6'1", 100-kilo bruiser probably helped, but really, it's about trust, and talking with people.

Unfortunately, the mentally ill rarely give you that option, and that's why many police officers find them hard to deal with.

I think we struggle to understand mental illness, individualy and as a community. Way too late in my career, another policeman gave me a perspective that I took to every subsequent contact with the mentally ill. He told me that we have these filters in our minds that cut out all the useless information we hear, see, smell and feel, things like an airconditioner humming in the background or the itch your clothes give you when you first put them on. He felt that people suffering from mental illness don't have the benefit of those filters, and are therefore constantly assaulted by these little noises and smells without a mechanism to drop them from their sensory input. He reckoned, and I agreed with him, that this situation would totally distract anyone from what is going on around them, and that this would be incredibly hard to live with.

To me that would be terrifying. He isn't a doctor, and I

don't know if he's right, but it, at least, made me think about how the mentally ill see the world and the police. Either way, it gave me pause and a new perspective.

CHAPTER 3

How to amputate a leg

What I did on my holidays

It was 2005, and I was still an operational police officer in Melbourne. I had agreed to help my mates at Australian Aid International if there was a disaster and we could help. On October 8 that disaster occurred — 86 000 thousand people were killed in Kashmir, Pakistan. The earthquake's epicentre was remote and straddled the contested Line of Control with India. Kashmir itself had been off-limits to outsiders for years and had been the scene of terrible fighting in the past. These were exactly the circumstances where we thought Australian Aid International could help. I took leave from the police and packed my bags.

This story is about Pakistan, and AAI's response to the Central Asian Earthquake. Really though, it starts in Melbourne, at the commandos. I used to listen to my mate Frank as he talked about doing aid work. He always had interesting stories to bring back from Africa or Bosnia, wherever the latest humanitarian disaster had erupted, where he had been chased down the side of a mountain by bandits, or bluffed his way through checkpoints armed by rebels. It was exciting stuff and, as far as I was concerned, he was saving lives and changing the world.

He was able to talk about the things you saw in the news and depicted in movies: the UN, geopolitics, atrocities, and war zones in far-off places. Frankly, who wouldn't want to do that?

Frank could see a number of parallels between the skills aid workers required in these situations and the skills soldiers like the commandos had. Commandos operate in rough conditions, far from assistance, in dangerous circumstances and many commandos are expert medics. They seemed like perfect candidates for the new extreme environments in which aid workers operate. His mind was ticking over and telling him to start his own NGO, and get his network of mates from the army to help. He got together with another friend, Marc Preston, who was a lawyer and businessman with a similar view, and formed Australian Aid International. I agreed to help, and then the earthquake occurred.

My phone rang. It was Frank.

'Well, Nathan, are you going to come and save lives or sit at home rearranging your sock drawer?'

Frank loves this expression and it seems to have the right combination of appealing to your machismo and emotional blackmail that gets people across the line, and overseas.

At the time Frank called me with the famous dare-to-work-for-us speech, one of my mates was with me, a cartographer who worked for Lonely Planet guidebooks. He wished he could come along, but had no medical experience or army training. I rang Frank back and soon my mate Paul was sitting next to me on that plane to Pakistan. I told Paul's wife I wouldn't let anything happen to him and she just raised an eyebrow and gave me a look—she knows me pretty well. We needed all the help we could get and Paul, my mate, would soon prove vital to our operations.

I recall on the plane over to Pakistan Paul asked me about three times, 'Yeah, but what can we do, we're just a couple of guys?'

I'm sure a lot of people were thinking the same thing. I didn't really have an answer for him.

And so, having paid our own way to Kashmir, Pakistan, we soon found ourselves at a base camp in the Himalayan foothills. At the time AAI operated with totally self-funded volunteers from our pool of mates. Those who could would drop everything, buy an air ticket to the disaster area, show up and run complex operations. It sounds ridiculous, but works amazingly well. We have all readjusted our lives around deploying to disasters as they occur.

The house we operated out of was a half-collapsed summer resting chalet for the Pakistani military. It sat on a hill that's higher than any point on mainland Australia. We nicknamed our new humanitarian base the Eagles Nest after a famous house that Hitler owned on an alpine peak in Germany. The irony of the Eagles Nest being a humanitarian base was not lost on us. It made me smile every time I heard it.

We had a few doctors with us, mostly American emergency specialists who were great guys. They had volunteered at the outset of the emergency, and cheerfully landed in a foreign country where Americans just aren't that welcome. They trusted us to get them in and out safely and point them to casualties. Our operations in AAI basically revolved around delivering the doctors to the patients. Simple. We broke up into medical teams and went to remote areas to help treat the thousands of people injured by the earthquake.

I had carried out all manner of medical procedures while I was in the commandos. On the medical course I had completed in the army, we trained to immediately assess a casualty, find the life-threatening injury, and diagnose and treat the problem. We studied the body and its systems and practised our craft in hospitals around the capital cities. We could take blood, give fluids and intravenous drugs and medicines, carry out simple emergency surgical procedures and keep people alive. We could set bones, open airways or create new ones if need be, prepare patients for evacuation and generally deal with most injuries that can occur on the battlefield. Disasters weren't much different.

The medical course was hard. The study and exams were tough and every day we poked cannulas into each other's arms to prove we could find the vein, injected local anaesthetic into body parts to get a feel for the effect, and stuck tubes down each other's throats into our stomachs for a reason that was never satisfactorily explained. Anyway, it was a great course.

I remember one of the first patients I had at a Sydney hospital was a 15-year-old girl. She had been fainting and feeling generally unwell. All my experience dealing with special forces soldiers, all male and at the peak of their fitness, didn't really help. I checked my army-issued medical manual and predictably it didn't mention fainting spells in 15-year-old girls. After a long conversation where I thought I had asked her everything that could possibly be wrong, I had two incredibly insightful recollections about 15-year-old girls, one of which just had to be the problem—15-year-old girls menstruate and can be pregnant! Nope and nope, as it happens. I was clearly stumped. In the end it turned out she was stressed about upcoming exams. There were obviously quite a few gaps in my knowledge.

That wasn't the end of my medical training though. While I was in Pakistan with the army I was lucky enough to work with a very special doctor. His name is Larry Stock, and he is an incredibly experienced emergency medical technician from America. He is infectiously enthusiastic and utterly indefatigable. Better than this, he is a great teacher. He taught me a number of important lessons and showed me crucial medical techniques. He would grab you at 10 PM if you had a spare hour, or in the back of some truck on a long journey, and proceed to teach, on notebooks and improvised teaching aids made of pieces of bamboo and rubber tubing. He had a way of explaining medicine that laid bare the human body and artfully showed the path out of trouble. He stood beside you and had confidence in you, and you, in turn, had confidence. He taught me to amputate a leg. It was an important lesson.

So, I found myself in charge of a small medical team in the foothills of the Himalayas. I was lucky enough to have another American doctor with me who was a real outdoorsman, fit and hard. He had climbed many of the large peaks in Colorado in the last few years and was no stranger to carrying a pack. It is always the individual abilities of your team members that lend you flexibility in operations. Knowing the doctor's abilities I planned my trip to a fairly difficult area, where no other medical team could really operate. There were other medical NGOs working in the area, but most of them ran large hospitals.

This meant that if the patients could not get to these hospitals, they would not get treated.

We got the Pakistani military to fly us in a Bell UH-1 helicopter higher into the mountains to our northwest, and drop us off. The Pakistani military were great to work with. They were very professional and eager to help. They had suffered enormous casualties themselves, when a number of their barracks had collapsed. They still had huge tasks ahead of them and tried to work as best they could with a mishmash of the world's humanitarian population, who had descended into remote, contested Kashmir.

The plan was to spend a few days walking across a couple of ridges and treat the people in otherwise inaccessible villages. We would stay overnight in the villages, where it was safe, and then move on the next day. People who had been well enough to make the long walk down to a hospital had reported that there were many injured people still in the villages. We felt we had enough information to mount a trip up into these distant villages and attempt to treat the injured, or arrange for them to be picked up by chopper and flown down to the hospitals.

Everything was going really well. We treated hundreds of people and had a number of serious casualties evacuated to hospital. Many people had broken bones and I lost count of the amount of limbs we straightened and put in casts. Our packs were getting lighter every day and we were making our way down to a place where a Pakistani helicopter would pick us up. These were some of the most beautiful places I had ever seen, and many of the villages we visited had not had Westerners in them in living memory. This area had been off-limits to foreigners, and even to Pakistanis who were not locals, basically since Pakistan was formed in the 1940s. So you can imagine the reaction of the locals when three bedraggled Westerners walked into their villages, wearing packs full of medical supplies. Actually, after a day or so working in this area, people we would meet while walking obviously knew us by reputation and usually stopped us to shake hands. We could not speak to each other, but I knew what they were saying.

Paul and I had been in Pakistan for a couple of weeks and had to go back to our real jobs in the next few days. That meant we had to get a helicopter back to our base and then leave soon after that. It was going to take a few days to get out of Pakistan. Jim, the mountain-climbing American doctor, would leave the mountains a few days later, from a different village, a short walk away, where he would conduct a small clinic by himself. He would not have to travel very far, and we had already been to that village, so we were happy with the arrangements. The helicopter that was picking him up would be too late for Paul and myself. I was meant to be back in a police uniform, taking phone calls, in about three days, so didn't have a moment to spare.

We had seen about 30 patients in a really remote village on the last clinic day for Paul and me. This was the furthest we intended to walk and from here we would turn back towards where we had come from and make our way to the helicopter RV (rendezvous).

In this area you could see K2, the famous Himalayan peak. It was obviously very rough terrain and we couldn't go anywhere in straight lines, but had to contour around huge mountain ridges and peaks that towered above us and blanketed us with shadow in the early afternoon. Walking with our heavy packs full of medical gear and sleeping bags etc. was still pretty hard. I was looking forward to the return journey and so was our guide, a local guy we had picked up along the way.

Our guide did not speak any English and my Urdu is frankly not as good as it could be, since I can only say about three words, so that was a slight problem. Not as much as you think, though. Every time we found somebody who spoke English we would get him to confirm our plan with the guide. The guide carried a big pack too, and was like a machine when it came to trekking up there in that rarefied air. He was old and hard and wore shoes that were made from one piece of moulded soft plastic, modelled to appear like brogues or formal Western-type shoes. We called them 'go-fasters'. These guys didn't wear socks. Socks are for girls, apparently. All the local guys wore these shoes and I was ready to trade in my $300 hiking boots and get a pair if it would make me as fast and stable as these guys in the hills. Something tells me it was not just the shoes though. Perhaps it was the chain-smoking and missing teeth that gave him his special hill-climbing powers. If so, I might give those training techniques a miss.

Anyway, we were packing up so we could start our long hike to the RV when an older bloke came up and sat off to the side. I call him a bloke, but it would be more appropriate to call him a gentleman. He was dressed very neatly in traditional clothes in the local style, but wore no headdress. He had a few extra adornments like a bracelet and necklace and was erect and proud even while seated. He looked pretty well fed for a man living in these parts, and I knew from the first moment I saw him that he was an important local character. I looked over to him and nodded a silent hello in his direction. He said, 'I see you are busy, sir, so I won't take much of your time.'

I was taken aback by his perfect English and extraordinary politeness, given the circumstances. I stopped packing up and gave him my full attention.

'Not at all, sir, how can we help?'

He stood up and now came forward.

'I am sorry that I was not here before you ended your clinic here. I had hoped that you might be able to help me. Though, now I have been informed by your guide that you must return to another village, so I will let you go.'

He looked well enough to me. He was about 45 years old and appeared to be in quite good health, strong and fit.

'Ok then, sir, well, good luck.' I shook his hand and nodded a goodbye as I was turning away. At other times I would have liked to have a nice conversation with the man, find out his circumstances and why he had travelled to the clinic, even though he was well.

The man nodded in reply and was about to walk away then stopped.

'There is one way you may be able to assist me if you have just a few minutes.'

I was lifting a heavy pack onto my back as he spoke, but the expression on my face obviously encouraged him to continue.

'I have to amputate my son's leg, and would like some advice from you on how to perform the operation.'

Well, suffice to say he had my absolute and undivided

attention. I called out to Jim, who came over, and we listened to the man explain that the collapse of a house during the earthquake had badly injured his 10-year-old son's leg. He believed that the leg was no longer viable and that infection would soon kill his son if he did not remove it. He reasoned that his house was too far away for us to travel to and perform the amputation ourselves, and therefore he had resolved to do it himself, with some advice from us.

This man had made a terrifying and difficult decision, the responsibility and weight of which must surely be crushing him. I can't imagine the position I would have to be in to make that choice about my child's limb. The earthquake caught a lot of people inside houses, as it happened at about 8 AM when people were preparing food. There were many terrible crush injuries as the houses, particularly the roofs, in that part of the world were very heavy, built, as they were, to withstand the heavy snowfalls of winter. They were not built to be earthquake proof.

We asked the man where his village was and how long it would take to get there. Of course, our problem was that Paul and I had to meet a chopper that afternoon, because we knew it was scheduled to land at a village not too far away. Walking to this guy's son would take us away from that, and effectively make it impossible to meet our helicopter. Itching the back of my brain was the promise I had made to Paul's wife, so I discussed it with him. It would mean we would probably have to use all the next day to walk down through a long valley we could see stretching off in the east. There was an NGO operating in the end of that valley that we had been in close contact with. Ange, an American friend of ours, was there, and could arrange transport to get us back in time. The other problem was that there was only one guide, and I would send him back with Jim, so we would have to navigate our own way out. This could be a problem, but I was pretty confident that the village trails would lead exactly in the direction we were going – there was nowhere else to go, really, because climbing the sides of the mountains in the valley would be horrendous. So I thought we would be OK, and told Paul this. Paul was into it. He showed a lot of courage to do that, and had impressed me with his fortitude on a number of occasions. Plus, nobody wanted to think about this old man cutting off his son's leg.

So we started the walk. Now, you always have to be a bit circumspect in situations like this when locals tell you something is not far or will only take a short time. I'm convinced they are not being deceitful, but are just wildly inaccurate or have an entirely different system of reference for what is near or far. Too bad, we were going anyway.

In this case it was about three hours of hard hiking. Very steep terrain that I never wanted to have to cross again. In fact I felt sorry for Jim, who would have to return along this route.

It transpired that the old boy had been educated in England and had returned home and was quite a wealthy landowner, in a relative sense. He had seven houses and a great deal of livestock. He told us that he had a grain mill at his house that was powered by a river that flowed through the edge of his land. He did, however, live in a highly remote, if picturesque and fertile, place and that was a disadvantage, especially today.

He said his son had not walked since the earthquake, but

on questioning he said his son was otherwise well. At this stage the earthquake had occurred about three weeks previously. Usually with a person with a bad injury that required amputation, three weeks after the injury they would be in a very bad way. So the fact that he was not generally sick was a good sign. Jim and I were going through a mental inventory of everything we would need to treat the kid. We went through all the options, from amputation onsite (our last option and only if there was immediate danger to the life of the boy), to evacuating the kid to a place where we could arrange a helicopter to fly him to hospital.

We thought we were reasonably well prepared, at least mentally, for whatever would confront us. Weeks of seeing kids in pain, with terrible injuries, had got us comfortable with the mental insulation that is required to do this sort of thing. Sometimes there were so many injuries, not to mention deaths, and so little you could do to improve the situation that you have to have your head right before you start. The overriding rule of first aid — Do no harm — is always there and anything we could do to help is something these people would never have got otherwise. As I walked along I tried to remember all the anatomy of the leg and thought about how I would assist Jim in whatever had to happen next. I did not want to perform an amputation on a 10-year-old boy on the side of a mountain in Pakistan. That much I knew for sure.

PROCEDURE FOR AMPUTATING LEG

Planning—The first point to consider, when you're about to amputate a limb, is where. You are attempting to remove the non-viable limb which is threatening the life of the patient, but still maintain as much of the limb as possible. In the case of the leg this is especially important. Do you amputate above the knee, forever robbing the patient of that important articulated joint, or below, allowing much more flexibility in the choice and use of a prosthetic limb?

The first incision—You make what is called a fish-mouthed cut around the bone. Imagine drawing a big open fish mouth on the side of your leg, with the mouth open towards the extremity of the limb. This allows you to keep as much tissue as possible to ultimately wrap around and act as a cushion for the bone.

As you cut into the leg you come across a number of large arteries and veins. These have to be dealt with carefully. They have to be tied off but left so that they allow as much blood perfusion as possible to the end of the limb. This is dangerous, as ligating (tying off) these arteries is a delicate process and can obviously cause terrible bleeding. The legs are full of large muscles and therefore massive arteries carry the required blood for functionality. You cannot afford to damage these vessels.

VIABLE TISSUE

Once you have cut deeply into the leg, down to the bone, and have carefully dealt with the arteries and veins, you need to pull back the lower and upper parts of the fish mouth and expose the bone. You need to keep as much muscle in place as possible, but make sure you remove all of the infected area. You have laid the bone bare and now have to cut it. (We carried Jiggly Saws, the wire cable cutting device like the ones used in survival kits to cut wood. These are great for cutting through bones.) You need to cut through the bone high up, away from the ends of the tissue, like a tongue deep inside the fish's mouth. This allows you to fully enclose and pad the bone with the viable tissue that is left.

Then you need to stitch the two halves back together. Care has to be taken so the correct tension is applied to the two halves of the tissue remains, so that they do not come under stress and pull apart as the tissue swells and readjusts itself after the surgery.

––––––––––––––––––

Of course, we would also be contending with the already diminished health of the boy, the unsanitary conditions on the side of a mountain in Pakistan, the existing infection in the leg, working through an interpreter for everything we required the patient or family to do, and our limited resources and time.

You can see why carrying out this procedure was weighing heavily on our minds and why I wasn't really looking forward to what would greet me in the village.

Oh, if you are planning a home-style amputation, please at least consult the internet for more definitive advice before proceeding. Just kidding. Do not do it!

Well, they sent a runner ahead to prepare the boy for us to treat him. We walked the final stretch through a magnificent valley, long green grasses lined the ground, and the area was wooded with huge trees and many cows grazed lazily, relatively unmoved by our approach. The man told us that the land and animals were his. In this part of Pakistan he really was a rich man.

When we got to the village the boy had been carried out on a bed and placed on the roof of the grain mill, which was the only level piece of ground within the little collection of houses. The whole family had gathered around. Shy little girls heralded our approach to the assembled family members and hid from us once we got up close. I'm sure I winced in anticipation as I walked up to the boy. The boy looked at Jim and me like we had fallen from outer space and fireworks were going off behind our heads. He was very frightened, and fair enough, as I bet he had been told we were there to amputate his leg.

I looked down at his leg and immediately shot a shocked look at Jim, who did the same. There was a 15 cm × 10 cm wound on the boy's calf, but no broken bone, no significant loss of tissue, or muscle, and ABSOLUTELY NO REASON TO AMPUTATE. I reckon I nearly cried. I have never been happier not to have to use my training. In fact the wound was healing by itself and was certainly not infected. If you wanted a picture of a wound healing itself for a textbook, you could have used this kid's leg as a model. I was absolutely rapt. Only Paul still looked and sounded aghast, and what did he know, he drew maps for a living. I think he had heard us doing our preparation out loud for the last few hours and still thought the worst.

We explained the situation to everyone and the mood got much happier. Of course, we still treated the boy's leg, but only with nice sterile dressings, some cream and antibiotics. The situation was very strange. I was at once relieved that we were not about to perform surgery, and at the same time felt stunned by the terrible consequences that would have befallen the boy had his father carried out his own plan of home amputation. I wondered how many other home-style surgical interventions had been carried out in the weeks following the earthquake.

We gave the old man about three weeks' supply of dressings and cream and had a look around our idyllic setting. Even the little girls lost their shyness and came to look at our curious belongings. I always carry balloons for the kids in these situations, and have for years. They're perfect. You can squeeze a heap of them into a little space or pocket, every kid in the world loves them, and you know very well that they will soon break, so you can be the good guy the next time you come, too. Ha-ha, classic hearts and minds theory!

The river that ran through the land was beautiful and clear and slipped through a series of small rapids and waterfalls as it rushed past. There was a beautiful dense forest on the other side of the river, and the trees continued, tightly spaced, up the side of the hill right up to the snowline.

The old man got the plumbing going to show us how the grain was milled by the large stone being spun on a spindle powered by the river. We sat down, again on the roof of the mill, and had a great meal of beef and rice and a few pieces of flat bread made right there. Flat bread has never tasted so good to me. I was very content to have missed my helicopter, and felt very much appreciated by these people. Most of the time while we were in these remote villages, they fed us. They had very little, but gave what they did have to us. Effectively, we could never carry enough food for ourselves and all the med supplies we needed, so it was a good arrangement.

I was pretty bloody happy with myself for making the effort to walk over and treat this kid, even if it meant a long walk out. Too bad! I slapped Paul on the back for the hundredth time since realising we would not be amputating any legs and got ready to go. I couldn't stop smiling. I reckoned we could still make it down the valley to Ange's camp by nightfall, but it would be close. Jim and the guide got ready to head back over the ridges we had crossed, and we took some of the heavier stuff we hoped he wouldn't need. It was basically a downhill journey, at last. We said goodbye to Jim, the boy and the rest of the people in the village and started our long walk out.

The path at the bloke's village was really in good shape, and I reasoned that it would only get better as it wound its way past other small villages towards a more built-up area. I thought we would make good time. As we took our first steps the father came out with an old shotgun and tried to give it to me. He told me that tigers come down out of the forest at night and I should take it for protection. He had an AK47 assault rifle too, but needed to keep that one. I thought that the sight of an armed white guy walking down through the valley in Kashmiri

Pakistan might ruffle a few feathers and, frankly, get me killed faster than any tiger, so I declined.

It was a hell of a walk, but all downhill and powered by our own sense of self-satisfaction, which is a pretty good fuel source. Paul and I got a good chance to talk on that long walk and we were pretty much sold on the idea of Australian Aid International. That kid, and the old man, learnt quite a few do's and don'ts of medical procedures from us, but I learnt something from that kid too. Sometimes, the efforts of a few individuals do make a huge difference.

Needless to say we made it home. Well, I did, a tiger got Paul. Just kidding.

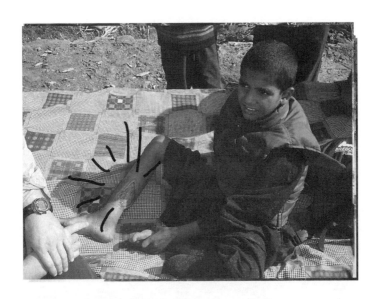

These girls steered clear of us – fair enough, they thought we were going to amputate their brother's leg.

CHAPTER 4

The only thing we have to fear is fear itself.
That, and white-tailed spiders.

The closet claustrophobic

I want to talk about fear. We let it hold us back too much. Fear is a funny thing. I always think of it as a disease: it is natural, evolves with society, it can affect any of us at any time, everyone has different tolerances and triggers, and it is infectious. Of course, you will get over it, and it is treatable. Sounds like a disease to me.

The other thing about this subject is that very often we mix up definitions. For example, being brave and being unafraid are very different things. My mate Campbell hates military parachuting. He really hates it. It scares the crap out of him, but in the commandos we all have to do it as part of our special forces training. I remember the night before his first jump he was out of his head. He ran around flipping tables over and screaming. He didn't sleep a wink. Did he jump the next day? Of course he did. He's brave. It scared him, but he was brave. That's what we require of soldiers.

Take me, on the other hand. When I think about military parachuting I don't get images of plummeting to the ground and bouncing 2 metres in the air before coming back down looking like a plastic bag full of sheep guts. I'm more worried about the highly uncomfortable and restrictive harness I have to wear. Am I brave? No. I am unafraid, and that is entirely different. The Army's Parachute Training School has a very famous motto: Knowledge Dispels Fear. I agree with that. Or, at the very least, it helps me. They go to a lot of effort making sure you are confident in the reliability of the equipment. I appreciate that, and that knowledge, to a high degree, does dispel my fear. At the Parachute Training School you watch them pack parachutes, you have a presentation on the materials they use, watch videos and live demonstrations, and then begin your training. At the end of that, your new knowledge has dispelled a great deal of your fear.

Brave is recognising something that really scares you, something that makes you feel like you're sure to be injured or killed, and still doing it, because you're motivated. You feel like you need to do it and, having full knowledge of the risk to yourself in doing it, still go ahead and do it. Doing something out of sheer desperation, to save your own skin, is not brave, it's a natural survival instinct. That's different.

Here's a great example from when I was a kid. My class at primary school went on an excursion to the Yarra River in Victoria. The river is a Melbourne landmark, and is deep and fast-flowing most of the time. I was about twelve years old and messing around with my mate Dino, too close to the edge. Dino fell in, of course. I say of course because Dino couldn't swim. I could swim, so I didn't fall in. That's just the way life is. I watched Dino for a few seconds as he thrashed around and never got his head above the water to get a breath of air. He was getting lower and lower in the water. He was drowning, and I knew it, and the few other mates that were standing around just yelled at him to swim or ran around in circles panicking. That's what you do when you're a kid.

I jumped in and swam over to Dino. I dragged him towards the edge of the river and tried to grab the muddy bank. One of our mates reached down and I grabbed his hand. We got pulled out of the water. No big deal. It was a summer day and reasonably warm. I was only in the water for about a minute anyway. Any other time, on a day like this, I would have spent an hour messing around in the water with my mates, and loved it.

Our teacher came over to tell us off, then took me aside and told me that it was a very brave thing I just did. When we got back to the school the principal told me the same thing (including telling me off). I didn't agree that I was brave, and I still reckon I was right. I was never in any danger and no real great physical effort was required on my part. What I did was not brave, just a bit inconvenient, as I got soaking wet in my school uniform. If I had been terrified of the water and barely able to swim but still jumped in, then sure, you could call that brave. But that just wasn't the case.

Observing fear in other people, and how it develops, can be really instructive. It can give us an insight into how we might react, given the right circumstances (actually, they are the wrong circumstances, if they make us scared), and we can file that away to avoid that behaviour. I don't know about you, but watching scared people really disconcerts me. When they're scared I start to think that maybe I should be scared too.

One day I was doing a military parachuting series in Victoria in the Army Reserve commandos. We were taking off from Avalon Airfield and flying out over Port Phillip Bay, then parachuting down into the ocean. Once we hit the water, other soldiers, who had already jumped, would pick us up in a small boat. It was pure commando stuff and I loved it. The commandos are meant to be a large-scale raiding force that can attack from a long distance, because they can fly in, be dropped by parachute into the ocean, get boats ready and then drive the boats the rest of the way to the target area. In the 1st Commando Regiment we were all reservists, so we did this sort of training when we could while still holding normal jobs or studying. To me, parachute jumps into water are even easier than land jumps because you can't get blown onto nearby roads or buildings or any of that crap. So, no worries.

We were jumping out of the rear cargo door of a Hercules c-130 aircraft and I was scheduled to be last out of the plane. That means I have to get in first and walk all the way to the front of the plane. I was with a friend of mine, Dutchie. Dutchie is the nickname given to any person in the Australian Army who has a German name. He would parachute out just in front of me, as the second last man. Dutchie is massive. He's about 6'4" and built like a lumberjack. That's because in his day job he is a lumberjack. He builds incredible log houses, and works everyday in the outdoors swinging an axe or chainsaw. Well, he doesn't swing the chainsaw, I hope. He is also a highly experienced commando, and an established tough guy. He was an instructor on my recruit course when I joined the commandos, and would regularly chide us while we stood at attention at morning parade for not getting into as many fights and punching as many heads as he had the previous night. He was hard as nails and larger than life. Dutchie is also a thinker, a reasoned political debater, is generous and a good and loyal friend.

Anyway, often there are observers who come along for a ride in a plane and to see the commandos parachute. On this day two giggly girls, who look about 19 years old, come along for a bit of a thrill. They are in army uniforms but look like kids to me. At the time I'm about 26 and Dutchie is about 33. We don't see many female soldiers at the commandos, as there are no females serving as special forces soldiers. I don't know what unit they came from, but they are quite lucky to have this opportunity. Or so they think. They need to be right out of the way when people start racing down the plane and jumping out the back ramp, or they could get knocked over, or out, which would really suck. So they sit up near the front. Dutchie and I take our seats, which are just cargo nets that fold down from the side of the plane. We sit down and say hello to the girls, shouting over the fast revving plane engines. The enormous back ramp on a c-130 stays down throughout the entire procedure so there is noise and wind and the smell of aviation fuel all through the plane. Dutchie and I sit opposite one another and belt ourselves in with this ancient-looking buckle system that is used over the top of our reserve parachutes, slung from our midsection. One girl is sitting next to me, the other next to Dutchie, and he and I face each other.

Because we sit down first, while the other parachutists are still filing into the plane, I'm sitting back watching everyone else take their seats and fix their belts as the plane jolts and begins to taxi down the runway. I'm going through the parachute safety drills in my head and then look across at Dutchie and he is stony-faced. He has his fingers splayed across his reserve parachute and says it. The words nobody ever wants to hear when you're about to jump out of a plane.

'Nathan, this doesn't feel right. Something's wrong.'

Well, that gets my attention. The two girls too. They are both staring at Dutchie now and have shut up, quickly dropping the excited conversation they had been having.

I don't reply. I can't think of anything to say, frankly. Dutchie has been parachuting for years and, in my experience, is confident and calm. He's one of the guys who seem to enjoy parachuting. The next time he speaks he really raises his voice and it has that shrill panicked note that betrays deep fear and panic in a man.

'This is not fucking right! Get me out of here, Nath!'

I don't know what to say or do. This is a scene I thought I would never see. Dutchie is losing it. Dutchie starts tugging at his parachute harness and I reach across with what I think will be a calming gesture. He swats my hand away. The plane is taxiing down the runway now at a fair speed, bouncing around and really noisy.

'Leave me alone! I'm fucking getting off! You can all die, not me.'

I'm really perplexed. Refusing to parachute is just not on. You don't refuse. If you refuse to jump, you're out, that's it, leave the unit this minute. I can't believe what I'm seeing and I look at the girls, who are ashen-faced and have eyes like polished dinner plates. They're ready to get out too.

'Fuck! This fucking parachute is so tight I can't breathe.'

He looks like he's hyperventilating. He's really pulling at his harness, with no actual effect on loosening it, and he's squirming around in his seat. It looks like he's trying to stand up against the resistance of the seatbelt but obviously can't. The plane is also picking up speed, and there is just no way Dutchie can get off at this late stage in the game. I know this and quickly wonder how I can calm Dutchie's nerves, or, alternatively, think of a method of restraining this rampaging lumberjack. Frankly, nothing is coming to mind. His hands thrash at the buckle but he's not getting it undone.

'Fuck! This thing is jammed! I can't fucking get it off! Help me!'

'Dutchie! It's going to be fine, mate. Calm down.'

I'm raising my voice to try to break into his little self-made mental cocoon, but still don't want to alert every other person on the plane. This will end Dutchie's military career if he doesn't get back in control right now. But raising my voice against the noise of the engines and the bouncing plane doesn't seem to be working.

We're now hammering down the runway, speeding up for a take-off.

The girls are now officially freaked out. There are tears running down the face of one and the other one seems to be doing some sort of self-affirmation ritual. Probably, 'I want to go home. I want to go home.'

Not going to happen, love. We're all going for a nice little joy flight, except I'll be leaving the plane at 1000 feet, via the massive rear door.

Dutchie finally tears off his belt as the plane is about to get airborne. He yells, 'I'm getting out of here!'

The plane jolts into a really steep angle and climbs as I grab hold of Dutchie. There's a madman loose on the packed plane and I'm really fearful of what will happen next.

These Herc pilots, even though they're the aeronautical equivalent to bus drivers, are usually frustrated fighter pilots. So, with this in mind, they really turn on a big performance whenever they get a chance. I once flew in a Herc so low, for ten minutes, that I swear we should have been stopping at red lights and pedestrian crossings. This case is really no different, but we're going up and I mean as fast and as hard as possible.

Then I see it. Dutchie has a huge smile on his face. You bastard! Hook, line and sinker. He's laughing as he retakes his seat while the plane is still on a steep climb. We look at the girls, and he says, this time in a much calmer voice, 'Hey, hey, it was just a joke. Everything's fine, ladies, really.'

Ahh, nope. Everything is not fine. The girls are inconsolable and still absolutely terrified. Soothing words are going to take a long time to fix this and we just don't have the time. They probably got onboard twenty minutes ago, with a little bit of trepidation, maybe first-time flyers, maybe a little nervous and excited about seeing the big commandos. I imagine them getting over their fears so they could have a look at parachuting up close. How exciting! Whatever confidence they did have when they first stepped on the plane was stolen by a 6'4" practical-joking lumberjack. Yeah, I reckon fear is infectious, even fake fear.

When I think about this incident I have this image of the girls in my head. One is sucking her thumb, rocking back and forth in her seat, and the other is rigid and hyperventilating. They probably weren't that bad, but they weren't relaxed and comfortable, that's for sure.

The order we have been waiting for gets yelled back to us, 'Stand up. Hook on.' It's time to attach our static lines to a cable overhead and get the hell out.

'See ya, ladies.'

We left them to enjoy the rest of the flight with the bus-driving fighter pilots.

We're meant to be scared of some things. Heights and high speeds come to mind. Even confined spaces. Though I suppose we deal with confined spaces a lot better because of all the time we spent as kids hiding under beds and in closets. Being scared of heights is fair enough. Humans are designed to take the impact of falling about 2 to 3 metres. That could happen anytime, when you were out hunting woolly mammoths back in the old days, or now, changing a light globe. Being up around 50 to 100 metres off the ground is not conducive to good health, and we know this innately. It is genuinely hard to fight against this innate knowledge and overcome these sorts of fears.

Speed is another good one. We have built up a sort of

immunity because of all the time we spend zooming around in cars, but we don't have to move too far out of our comfort zone to feel uncomfortable. Try driving really fast with your significant other, and see what he or she reckons. In my experience it doesn't work out that well. Ask a relationship counsellor; I reckon they'll be against it.

I was a senior constable stationed in Melbourne's western suburbs and we had a work experience kid at the station. He was about sixteen and thought he was king of the kids by hanging out with the cops for a week. The thing was, he was generally confined to the office for the period, and that would suck, I know.

I tell the supervising sergeant that we will take the kid out and drive around doing a few files, or ongoing investigations, and that's exactly what we do. All is going well, and the kid loves being out of the office. We go around to a few businesses and private residences and are pretty pleased with ourselves. We're just heading back and getting into the car when I hear over the radio that there is a hot, or urgent, job a few kilometres away. The response vehicle is heading there, but is a fair way off. I consider dumping the kid on the street, but think, nah, we'll just head that way at a steady pace and see what happens. It's not that urgent, so it'll be OK. However, all the stars are lining up. The job address is just off the freeway and we're just getting onto the freeway so it won't take us long to cover the few kilometres in between. At 100 kilometres per hour, a car goes 1 kilometre every 36 seconds (I bet that equation gets stuck in your head).

As we enter the freeway there's an update and the job

becomes more urgent. There's a member of the public struggling with a guy he has caught in his house. Ok. It's about 11 AM and the freeway is pretty clear, no wind and a nice bright sunny day. I put the foot down and very soon we're sailing along at a decent speed. We're in the outside lane and there are only a few cars on the road, and they're all over in the lefthand lane. That's encouraging, not that I need much encouragement, since you are actually allowed to speed as a police officer. Pretty soon we're doing about 210 kilometres per hour and the car is absolutely roaring from wind noise and the engine giving it everything. The flashing lights on the roof of police cars make a huge racket at these speeds, from the wind rushing around them. The car feels pretty stable though, and this piece of freeway is particularly smooth, so I'm quite relaxed at this speed. It's fairly unusual to be doing these sorts of extremely high speeds, but most general duties police officers get up there every once in a while. My partner is calmly writing notes on the running sheet, taking down details of the event from the description on the radio. I decide to talk to the kid in the back.

'Is this the fastest you've ever gone in a car, mate?'

No response. Nothing. He must have heard me. He's only 1.5 metres away. I snatch a glance in the rearview mirror and the kid looks like a starfish squashed into the corner of the back seat, trying to brace himself with all his arms and legs at once. He is totally unable to speak.

'I will mark that down as a yes then.'

It doesn't take much to get out of our comfort zone. That kid had been travelling at 100 kilometres per hour routinely for years and I bet he was never a bit scared. At 200 he was a limpet stuck in the back seat. If you wanted to move him just then, you would have had to pry him out with the jaws of life and 5 kilos of plastic explosive.

I reckon he would still sweat telling his mates about that.

Anyway, we were there pretty quickly, but the guy had already got away.

I suppose I have experimented with fear many times in my life. Maybe I'm an expert. I'll tell you one thing, it's better to be an expert in inducing it in others than scaring the crap out of yourself.

For a short time in my life, I did this terrible job, and I only did it because I was working with a mate from the army, so it was fun, sort of. It filled in some time while I was waiting to go into the police academy, after having been accepted to start training. I was about 27. Our job was to get inside airconditioning ducts and climb through them vacuuming. Now I can't actually believe that I agreed to do it. And, actually, it wasn't fun at all now that I think about it.

So, we had to clean the ducts in a large Melbourne hospital and it was an absolutely massive job. We would open the suspended ceiling on each floor and then identify the airconditioning duct. We would then find a suitable place and cut a man-sized hole in the duct. Then we would have one guy go into the duct and the other guy stay outside on a stepladder, feeding the vacuum hose and power cord for our light.

Obviously, we would take it in turns to be the man outside the duct and the man inside the duct.

It was a horrible job. The ducts in this hospital were also really long and narrow and became narrower as you got to the end. It started out about 50 cm × 50 cm and got so narrow towards the end that, eventually, you just couldn't get any further along. Obviously, you can't turn around in a duct like that, and you have to adopt a crawling method, called, rather too cutely, the Kitten Crawl. This is where you put your arms out in front of you, about half-extended, and then rest on your forearms. Then you get on your toes and raise your body so only the toes and forearms are touching the floor/ground/duct. Then you push forward, maybe 20 centimetres at a time. It was a slow process and physically demanding, too. It would routinely take us about 30 minutes to reverse out of the duct when we had gone as far as we could. Despite being inside the airconditioning duct, it was always hot, hard work.

Now, having your mate stuck in an overhead airconditioning duct is frankly too good an opportunity to resist. You had to play a practical joke or two. No choice, really. There was one joke that seemed never to get old. If you were the guy in the duct, even though you knew your mate would play this joke, it would get you. It was good because it was simple. It had that element we used to see in old horror films. That is, allowing what is left unsaid, or unseen, to really terrify. Let the viewer/ victim's own mind get them more scared than you ever could.

I will explain. Hospitals are dynamic and dramatic places. That's why *ER*, *Grey's Anatomy* and *House* are all based in them. All sorts of emergencies happen there, so your imagination runs wild when given a little push. Once inside the duct, you really can't hear much. You can hear your mate, because he can stand on the stepladder and talk to you, and obviously his voice travels straight to you. But you can't hear much else, and, remember, you also have a vacuum going that isn't exactly the latest super-quiet stealth model.

For this joke to be executed in the best possible way, you would have to wait until your mate was right at the far end of the duct, when he had a 30-minute reverse crawl to get out of the duct.

The way to start the prank off would be by having one side of an imaginary conversation, as if you were speaking to some official from the hospital administration. You would do this at just the right level for your mate to hear you speak, but not quite loud enough to hear everything you said. Something like, 'Oh really. What, right now? Well, what will you do with all the patients? Oh. But I can't just leave, my mate's in the duct. Which floor? Well, it just isn't that easy. He's a long way in.'

Then you leave that to percolate for a few seconds. Now's the time to stay cool. You will know that your mate has heard you if the vacuum and electrical cords have stopped being tugged into the duct. This signifies that he has stopped, and is listening to your conversation. When you're in the duct, you're always listening out for things your mate on the stepladder might say. So you can be pretty confident he heard.

Then you speak to him.

'Rob, they say there's a small fire downstairs. We have to leave, mate. They have it under control but they're evacuating everyone just in case. You better start coming out.'

Then leave it a few more seconds, maybe 30 seconds and then blast him. Make your voice a little bit more panicked. Leave the vacuum on so he can't really hear anything, other than the information you give him.

'Rob, there's a bit of a panic on here now. Get your arse out of there mate. I'm going to see what's happening. I'll only be a minute.'

Totally ignore any requests for information that he has, and go silent.

Give it a good two minutes.

'Rob, I'm back. Rob! Can you hear me? Rob!? Rob!?'

Betray a little panic in your voice. Turn off the vacuum now. Still totally ignore anything he says. Act as if you can't hear him.

'Mate, don't worry, it's a couple of floors down, on eleven. Mate, the stairs are jammed. I'll wait here until you're out, any-way.'

One more minute. Remember, Rob has a good twenty min-utes of crawling yet to be out. Turn off his light. That really turns up the heat on the joke. Use your panicked voice again.

'The power's gone out. Look, mate, hurry up. Everyone else from this floor is gone. We're the only ones left. Seriously, man. Hurry up.'

Give it a couple of beats then deliver the coup de grace. Use a weak, apologetic voice.

'Rob, I'm just going to go and have a look. I'll be around, don't worry.'

Then go silent. Nothing. You are his only conduit to the outside world (which he thinks is on fire) and no matter how many times he yells 'Are you there?', you are silent.

CLEANING

Even if you know that this is bullshit, even if Rob taught you how to do it himself, it's still scary. Your mind plays tricks on you. Suddenly you'll be hearing people running down the halls and faint screams. You tell yourself over and over that it's bullshit, but what if this time he isn't bullshitting?

It's hard, believe me. In the two weeks that I cleaned those ducts, I reckon we did that to each other four or five times. There were some golden moments. After about a week a real alarm went off somewhere in the hospital and I immediately went into bullshit mode.

'Rob, did you hear that?'

Of course he did. You can imagine the rest.

I discovered something else during that job. I'm not claustrophobic, pretty obviously, but I did have an episode.

I was deep into one of the last ducts. It was narrow and I had to go on a 45-degree angle to get a little bit more room to wedge my body along, as my shoulders were getting stuck at the front. Now this sucked and made progress fairly slow. Actually, it pretty much signified the end of the line for me. I really couldn't move any further along the duct, and certainly couldn't do any real cleaning.

Suddenly the duct shifted as if it had dropped on its supports about 2 inches. Wow. Now that was scary. I will live a full and happy life without ever knowing what it's like to be in a duct while it falls from a ceiling overhead onto an operating table during open-heart surgery or some such procedure.

I kept very still for a second, and then thought, 'Mate, that's a sign that this duct is finished.' I was still pretty stressed from the sudden drop and instability in the duct, and shifted my body to start the reversing procedure. That bodyweight shift was a huge mistake. I suddenly slid down until my shoulder rested heavily against the duct floor. Immediately, I realised I was stuck, with only my lower arm and leg able to find any purchase at all. My arm was pointing out to my front, rather pathetically. There wasn't much chance of either my arm or leg adding to my possible locomotion. This was no good.

Oh shit. Suddenly I could feel the duct squeezing me. It was tight around my chest and making it harder to draw breath. I looked at the top corner of the metal duct, which was only about 15–20 centimetres from my face and, right before my eyes, it pressed in much closer, to about 10 centimetres away. I thought, 'I'm going to be crushed in here.'

I stopped all movement, closed my eyes and tried to take a slow easy breath. With my eyes still closed I had myself a little think, not directly about the predicament of being stuck, but about what could be squeezing the duct. The answer was obvious, and should have occurred to me immediately. Nothing. Nothing could cause the duct to squeeze in and bear hug me like this. The voice in my head was pretty self-satisfied: 'So this is what claustrophobia is like. Bullshit, I'm not claustrophobic!'

I opened my eyes and saw an amazing sight. I watched as the duct retracted away from me, and the pressure on my chest decreased. The mind is a powerful thing. I tried to move and got about an inch. Good enough. They say the longest journey is started with the smallest…yeah, whatever. I crawled out.

POWERFUL STUFF

In the duct that day I learnt a great lesson about fear. You just need a few factors to conspire against you, and all of a sudden your perception of reality changes, and your own mind can work against you. Powerful stuff. Even better though, I learnt to beat it, with reason.

Oh, I don't actually have any stories about white-tailed spiders, but they are scary, aren't they?

CHAPTER 5

You can't judge a book
by its multiple rows of flesh-ripping teeth

Just because it's called a shark,
doesn't mean it will eat you.

Don't judge a book by its cover. All that glitters is not gold. Or, if you're into Sigmund Freud, a cigar may actually be a penis. The point here is that not all is as it appears, and that our perceptions of an event may be marred by inaccurate or incomplete information that other people have given us. I love old sea charts where the uncharted regions have a depiction of a huge menacing serpent or octopus and script underneath saying 'Here be monsters'. There were no monsters, but the cartographers didn't want to admit that they really didn't know what was going on there. So they just played to our fears and prejudices.

And so it is with sharks. The name shark is very evocative of man-eating killing machines, but it shouldn't be, really. The overwhelming, vast majority of sharks swim around and are quite happy never to eat a human. They love fish. That's how it is. This is even true of great whites. Great white sharks do not prefer to eat people over fish, or they would hang around Bondi Beach and Surfers Paradise and get fat and lazy very quickly.

Right now, they eat big fish, and seals and things, which, in comparison to humans, are quite hard to catch.

Don't get me wrong. I have a lot of respect for sharks. As a surfer and diver in the waters of southern Australia you tend to think about them a bit more than most people. They hold a special place in the psyche of all ocean users, and everyone thinks about them differently. I have no doubt that great white sharks and other species eat people, or even just give them a chomp to see how they taste. But it just doesn't happen often enough to worry about.

I reckon that when you decide to become a surfer (does anyone actually decide to become a surfer?) you have to accept certain realities. You will need to get pretty good at swimming. You will get sunburnt in summer and freeze in winter (down south anyway) and there is a small chance that you will have an encounter with a shark.

Imagine there was a game played in the African savannah. Maybe frisbee or chasey, where you ran around but could never really see where the dangerous animals were. Basically, you just blundered about thinking about the game and not your surroundings. I reckon, in the course of that game, you would occasionally run into a lion, and that lion would occasionally eat you. Now, if that happened, I don't think there would be a bunch of idiots the next day rushing through the savannah trying to kill all the lions. You were stupid enough to play in the lion's hunting area and you got eaten. Tough luck. You took a chance, knowing there was the possibility of meeting a lion, and he or she ate you.

However, that seems to be the way we feel about sharks.

NOT FAIR

If a shark eats somebody who blunders about in the shark's natural territory, the very area in which the shark is attempting to find food, then we go on an ill-directed rampage, trying to get the man-eater that is out there, threatening our freedom and very existence. It's not fair, and I reckon that as a user of the ocean there is a contract, admittedly unsigned, that if you get bitten, tough luck. It's extremely rare anyway. So rare that it's not worth worrying about. Anyway, there is NO sport or activity based in the ocean where shark bite is the biggest danger. None.

While I was in Papua New Guinea for the Australian Army I was stationed in a fairly remote village on the south of the island. The village, called Buin, was a quiet little place established on the alluvial flats at the base of a fairly steep mountain system. The area all around was basically covered in low jungle and swamps as you got closer to the ocean. Buin itself was about 10 kilometres from the ocean, and occasionally, about once every two to three weeks we would travel down a rough dirt road to the ocean for a swim in the cool waters of the Solomon Sea. I always looked forward to those trips and having a look around the beautiful coastline of Bougainville. Usually, most of the staff would head down for a swim, just leaving one or two behind to monitor the camp.

It was a multinational mission with members from Australia, New Zealand, Vanuatu and Fiji. There was a female medic in our group, Kahlia, who was from New Zealand. Anyway, whenever we all went for a swim in the ocean she would never go in the water. She would swim in the rivers near to our camp, but not the ocean. She was a good swimmer, just really scared of sharks. I felt sorry for her because she would come down, stand on the beach and swelter in the heat, watching us all having a great time in the water.

Before our next trip I decided to talk to her at length about sharks, trying to convince her that it was actually extremely rare to see sharks anywhere in the ocean, even in areas where sharks are prevalent, and that we had never seen any sharks at the beach, and the place where we swim wasn't really good shark habitat anyway, blah, blah, blah. It was a long talk.

The idea was to make her confident enough to get in the water and stop worrying about sharks. If I'm honest, I passed myself off as a bit more of a shark expert than I actually was, but I had good intentions, hoping to help her with her fears. Things were looking up. She seemed convinced, firstly of my expert knowledge of sharks, and secondly that there were no sharks at the beach where we swam.

So we took the long, hot drive down to the water. The day was particularly hot and steamy and I personally was dying to get into that water. We pulled the vehicles up on the beach and got out. I walked down to the water with Kahlia and we got to the water's edge. She still looked scared but seemed willing to have a go. She was trying and I respected her for that. I knew I was going to have to take it easy with her, and not push too hard. She gave me a worried look and said, 'Stay right next to me, please?!?!'

No worries. I was talking her in and everything was going

just fine. In about a minute she was standing in chest-deep water. She was just over a metre away from me and seemed to be enjoying herself. The water was clear and cool, and at the bottom we could see and feel the fine sand comfortably underfoot. She was talking and laughing and seemed pretty much at ease. As far as I was concerned, we had completely cured her fear of sharks. Well, at least a bit.

We stood there for a few minutes and then about five small fish, about 20 centimetres long, swam between us, right at the surface, obviously being chased by something, ahhh, bigger. Oh shit. I looked at Kahlia, and she was oblivious, probably thinking how great it was to see those cute little fish close up. I, though, had a good idea that whatever was coming, it was big enough to snack on 20-centimetre fish.

It only took a moment. The chaser swam right between us. It was a nice little reef shark, about a metre and a half long. Either of us could have reached out and touched it. Her eyes just about jumped out of her head. She opened her mouth and looked at me, as if to say, 'That was a SHARK, wasn't it?', but nothing came out.

I spoke up. 'Yes, Kahlia, that was a shark.'

I was smirking, as we weren't in any danger at all, but she didn't see the funny side of it. She hit me as she thrashed towards the shore and only stopped to turn around when she was about 10 metres up the beach. Whoops.

I have been in the ocean countless thousands of times, in the tropics, down in southern oceans, all over the world, and I can count on one hand the times I have seen sharks when I was not actively looking for them. Kahlia had been in the ocean about three times and a shark, in full-on attack mode chasing its lunch, comes within 50 centimetres of her. You can't help bad luck.

Of course, I would count that as good luck. We are lucky to have encounters like that with sharks, or any sea animals for that matter. It is a privilege, if you don't get eaten.

I have been lucky, or unlucky, depending on your perspective, with shark experiences.

I remember when I was about sixteen. The surf was flat and we decided to take my dad's Zodiac inflatable boat out to a reef off the coast. It was a beautiful summer day and perfect conditions for snorkelling. The two guys I normally surfed with were there and so was my older brother, Greg. Greg was about 26 at this time, and an extremely experienced diver and not afraid of anything in the ocean. He was always calm and confident and happily did things like wedging himself into underwater caves and sticking his hands into holes where I still would never stick anything.

The Ingoldsby Reef is awesome. It's a great site to dive, or even just swim around. I had been there countless times and always enjoyed searching this bit of ocean habitat. You could bring the boat into the lee of the reef at low tide and throw the anchor into relatively shallow water, or even drive right up to the exposed reef and drop people on it. The reef is an elongated oval and at the ends, unbroken waves swirl around and cause eddies and surging. It's great fun. The reef is now a marine reserve, which is a great idea, as it is teeming with abalone, crayfish and all manner of fish.

My mates and I had gravitated to this old boiler box, from a wreck, and would dive down and swim through it, just to warm up. The Box was a sort of initiation device that we used on new people when they came out to the reef for the first time. It was pretty confronting for a newbie. It was in about 4 metres of water and was about 3 metres long. It was encrusted with sea life and fish swam around in it. It was always interesting to see how new people coped with their first encounter. When you were wearing fins, it was actually really easy, but looked a bit sketchy from the entrance, or when looking down as you floated above, breathing up for your turn to dive The Box. It also had this dark and daunting feeling when you got up close and looked in, but really, like so many things that look scary, it was totally safe.

Anyway, when we got out to the reef, about a kilometre offshore, we anchored and started swimming around; it was about 3 to 4 metres deep. My brother had swum a little bit away, being a veteran of The Box, and was busy diving down and sticking his hand in crags and generally scaring the hell out of the local fish etc. when he suddenly broke the surface and yelled, 'Hey, there's a nice wobbegong here.'

Now, I don't know whether you know what wobbegong sharks are, but they are not going to win any beauty competitions, even if they are beautifully adapted to their environment. They are not the classic, sleek, grey shark of our worst fears. They are a mottled brown and sandy colour with a complex camouflage pattern, have a sort of flattened triangular body, an extensively flattened head and a broad mouth with a number of small appendages hanging off it. It's a forager around rocks, but is primarily an ambush predator, waiting for a prey animal, usually a fish, to swim past and then launching a quick attack from its concealed position. I would describe them as sort of a huge mottled catfish but that really isn't doing them any justice.

Wobbegongs are not particularly aggressive (to humans), but they lurk around the reef eating crustaceans and things they can catch, and sometimes come into contact with humans who are trying to do the same thing. Greg didn't seem terribly concerned about the wobbegong posing any threat. He seemed more excited than anything, so we swam over to have a look. Well, the shark was swimming in circles about 30 centimetres from the sea floor, which was covered in kelp, seaweed and rocks. Every ten seconds or so, he would plonk himself down into the seaweed, and the merits of his camouflage became obvious. He was pretty big, at least 1.5 metres or a bit more. I didn't know much about wobbegongs at the time (or now) but he didn't look that terrifying to me. He did seem to be a look-but-don't-touch prospect though.

As I was contemplating our observer-only status, Greg dived down and ran his hand down old Wobbe's flank then returned to the surface. The shark didn't move. That looked cool, and when he was back on the surface, Greg reported that the shark's skin was surprisingly rough. I was a little bit worried but family pride was on the line, so I dived down. As I was getting close I baulked because the shark decided to do another quick lap of the immediate area. His sudden movement had surprised me, and I was a bit wary for a second. He went in a circle of about 3 metres diameter and returned to the exact position he had been in previously. I put it down to bad timing and had another shot. No worries. He laid still and I got to confirm that his skin was, as reported, surprisingly rough. He may not have been pretty, but his strange looks were growing on me. He had a sort of purposeful look while he swam around, and then had a very reassured look when he stopped. The camouflage he was sporting really was a marvel; big though he was, he would have been easy to overlook because of it. I was certainly pleased to have had this chance to have a good close look at him.

Well, Craig and Pete, my two mates, also got to have a go of feeling the shark's skin. About this time Greg decided to go to the next level. He dived down and grabbed one of the shark's fins. The shark moved about a metre in a burst and then stopped. That looked cool too, but seemed to piss him off a bit, so I thought I might avoid that. I am sure both David Attenborough and Jacques Cousteau would agree with me there.

We were mainly floating around on the surface, watching Wobbe's antics and I got a chance to speak to Greg.

'Hey, Greg, do they ever attack?' I said while bobbing up and down.

'Nah, she's right.'

That was good news, all things considered.

So, next my mate Craig began his descent down to Wobbe just a second after Greg. The thing was, Greg decided to step it up a level and grab the shark in a kind of bear hug, well, shark hug, I suppose. Greg was trying to hold on but obviously Wobbe was not ready to move on to this stage in their relationship.

The shark did that twisting and squirming action you see on nature documentaries when they're feeding. I can tell you that it looked quite interesting from the surface, but I was glad to be nowhere near it. Ol' Wobbe had built up a head of steam but Greg was not letting go. Then Wobbe finally shrugged Greg off and sprinted away, or, at least, tried to. In an unfortunate quirk of timing and positioning, Craig was right there and blocking his path. The shark crashed straight into Craig's chest and then nudged down and swam between his legs and away to freedom. I could distinctly hear the peculiar squeal emanating from Craig. The best way to describe it is like an underwater scream. Craig moved like he had been electrocuted, shot and burnt at the same time. It is safe to say he got quite a surprise. Pete and I raised our heads out of the water, looked at each other and cracked up laughing. It was so funny I swear we nearly drowned. I was crying. Craig, to his credit, only took a couple of seconds to regain some sort of composure and join in.

That was the last we saw of Ol' Wobbe. I wonder how he recounts this story to his wobbegong mates.

When we got back to the shore we cleaned up, told the story to anyone who would listen and then I got out a reference book to check some shark facts. Among other things, I read, 'They may bite scuba-divers or snorkellers who poke or touch them, or who block their escape route.'

Nice one, Greg.

There has only ever been one time when I actually felt like I was going to be attacked by a shark. Actually, this should be considered strange because I have surfed in many places in Victoria where sharks are thought to be present. Lots of these places are what the assembled crew of experts refers to as a bit sharky. We actually use sharky as the adjective for describing a place thought likely to be inhabited by sharks. It might be sharky because of a nearby river mouth or local fishing industry or because many sharks have been caught or sighted in the area. Sometimes you would surf these places by yourself, or at dusk or dawn, when sharks are thought (by surfers at least) to be most active. Obviously, being by yourself increases your level of exposure to risk because you are the only red meat in the water. Also, the chances of survival in any emergency are lower because there is nobody there to help. Anyway, I have never seen a shark while surfing in one of these so-called sharky areas.

I had my most dangerous shark experience at a packed tourist beach, on a busy day in summer at about midday, with more than a thousand other people in the water around me. None of the usual factors existed to make this place or set of circumstances seem sharky in any way. I would have voted this the absolute least likely circumstances in which to see a shark, so, naturally, I see a shark. That's life.

I was about 22 and we had decided to surf at Fairhaven Beach on the Great Ocean Road near Aireys Inlet. This is a beautiful stretch of beach. Often enough at this time it was turning on some good surf, so we would always consider it a possible surf spot. The surf was actually crap on this day but we were desperate to get in the water because of the beautiful clear skies and inviting, cool ocean. The beach here stretches in a fairly straight line for about 3 kilometres and is a favourite place for families, and anyone, really, for a swim. There is a Surf Life Saving Club and the beach is very well patrolled. Our whole crew was there, having turned up in about three cars, and included were Craig and Pete, from the previous shark story, and some other mates. There were about eight of us in all hitting the water that day.

Now, it is extremely common to claim you might have seen a shark while surfing to scare the hell out of your mates. So you are always a bit circumspect about shark sightings by your mates in the water. You eye them suspiciously when you hear the report of their sighting and play a bit of psychological chicken. Of course, as the person making the fraudulent claim, you usually keep at least one level of 'I swear it's true!' in reserve, just in case it is true. It's best to be a little bit ambiguous and let their imagination do the rest.

'Mate, I'm not sure, I just saw a fin break the water over there behind you. It could have been a dolphin.'

The line above is for experienced or known bullshit artists. The emphasis is on the fact that 'it could have been a dolphin'. You don't even have to say the 'S' word. In fact, you didn't see anything, but you certainly never claimed to have seen a shark. Brilliant.

On this day I'm surfing near my friend John. He's a good surfer and not particularly easy to scare when it comes to sharks. He is, though, a prodigious, Gold Medal Class, A-Grade, Heavy Weight bullshit artist, so you eye anything he says with some amount of suspicion.

HANDIWORK

We're sitting on our boards about 150 metres out to sea. John is about 20 metres away from me and the rest of the crew is at least another 100 metres further away, down the beach. The day is perfect, except the waves are too small. The beach is as packed as the Victorian coastal beaches ever get. Looking left and right along the break there are at least a thousand punters in the water, and more than that on the beautiful white beach. The water has a crystal quality that, I can tell you, is very rare in Victoria. The overhead sunlight really penetrates down to the sea floor, maybe just over 3 metres below. Not many waves are coming through and I am well relaxed. We've been out for about an hour and all is well. We have had a good paddle around and cooled off and will probably head in soon.

Suddenly John says, 'Shit, Mullins, shark!'

I turn to face him and he furiously paddles like a mad-man and catches a tiny wave, which he belly-surfs all the way in to the beach. I am highly sceptical, but then two facts emerge, starkly, in my mind. The first is that if he was joking, he didn't stick around to admire his handiwork. Hmmm. Also, he belly-rode that wave all the way to the shallows, and no surfer spends all his time and effort waiting to catch a wave just to surf it in a straight line all the way to the beach...unless he is absolutely certain he doesn't want to drop off that wave in any circumstances. Hmmm. Hmmm.

I am guessing this is the real deal, or, at the very least, I should consider the distinct possibility. I immediately look down into the water around me, hoping to see nothing. Wrong. It takes me about 1 second to see it. A big box-headed bronze whaler slowly swimming right on the sandy sea floor towards me from the direction where John had been. Oh shit. He is as clear to me as if he was in a glass fish tank. He slowly rises from the sea floor like a jet taking off at the end of a runway and angles up towards me. Bronze whalers are fairly common around Victoria in summer. In fact, they seem to be pretty common all around the southern half of Australia. They are a big shark, and known and accepted as dangerous. They are not usually the classic grey colour of great white or reef sharks but are brown, sandy or, as the name suggests, a bronze colour. They have a sort of blunt-looking snout and a large mouth. Way too large for my liking right now.

There are not really many options for a guy on a little piece of fibreglass (it felt little then) with a shark coming up to get him.

Run! Well, paddle! I slap the water and do a half swivel so I'm facing the beach, then I dig my hands violently into the water to paddle towards the beach for all I am worth. I could easily have logged that time at the Olympic swimming trials as, I would suggest, I was fairly highly motivated. I immediately imagine the scene to follow with the shark accelerating towards me and slamming me off my board, then just nudging up, taking my leg in his mouth and pulling me underwater. No thanks. I can see the shark slowly cruising towards me and as my hands slap the water to paddle he does a lightning-fast 180-degree turn then slowly heads exactly along the path he came from. Then he turns to parallel me towards shore at a polite distance. Good enough for now, I'm outta there. I put in a few more big strokes and quickly lose sight of him. I don't mean that the pathetic speed I'm doing on the surface is fast enough to outrun him, I just mean he disappears from my sight. Maybe he doesn't enjoy the churned-up waters I'm paddling towards, maybe the violence of my initial strokes scared him. I don't know, but I do know that with every paddle stroke I can feel myself get safer and safer. I do not have the good luck John did and have to paddle most of the way to the beach before a decent wave comes through. I only feel safe in about knee-deep water and get off my board near where John is standing. We run down the beach to where the rest of the guys are surfing and stop to warn them by waving our arms above our heads.

I say to John, 'Do you reckon they've seen it?'

Just then you could see every one of them burst into frenzied activity and paddle towards the beach like they're trying to beat my Olympic time trial effort of a few moments before.

John says, 'Yep, I reckon they have.'

The shark alarm goes off as we stand on the beach and a bloke from the Surf Life Saving Club runs up to us.

'Hey guys, there's a shark out there. Don't go out.'

Thanks for the advice, mate.

There is chaos on the beach, and virtually nobody in the water. Ironically the surf has picked up a little bit. We walk back up to the cars and are patting each other on the back, they way you do when you feel like you have had a close call, and one of John's older brothers appears, having just donned his wetsuit, surfboard under his arm.

'Mate, there's a shark swimming around out the back, I wouldn't if I were you.'

He doesn't even stop. He just nonchalantly walks right

down to the water and goes for a surf. Hard as.

So yeah, sharks are not the villains they are made out to be. Oh, and it's not just sharks, in our modern world there are plenty of things that get demonised and become the scapegoat. It's the same as writing 'There be monsters' on those old charts because you actually aren't too sure what is really there. Take some time and make up your own mind about the monsters. There aren't that many out there.

The reality is that by far the greatest risk to surfers is skin cancer. However, skin cancer sightings rarely make the front page of the newspaper, or good subject matter for feature films. Sometimes we tend to ignore the real risks and focus on the sexy ones, to our detriment.

Of course, if I'm honest, Freud also said, 'Sometimes a cigar is just a cigar.' But then, as a major cigar smoker himself, he had to say that.

CHAPTER 6

29-year-old teenager

Can you prove you are sane? I can.

I feel like I have quite a few problems with maturity. Not with not having any, but with not wanting any. In nearly all circumstances in my life I have got along very successfully being imbued with what I think we, in Western society, call an immature attitude.

I'm not even sure what immaturity is. We throw that term around and use it to describe people's actions, usually with negative connotations, and maybe that's not fair.

Since I was eighteen I have nearly always had jobs that put me in a responsible position. Generally, I seek out positions of responsibility and authority and enjoy them very much. I have been in charge of large groups of people, managed complex projects, and been involved in intricate legal proceedings, in criminal and industrial relations courts. In the police, military, humanitarian and private enterprise worlds, I have repeatedly positioned myself in critical situations where good, sound decision-making and calm resolve were critical to successful operations and often lifesaving.

At the same time, I watch *The Simpsons*, would prefer a chocolate milkshake to a grown-up drink like coffee or alcohol, and love to ride the local BMX track on my single-speed jump mountain bike. I don't smoke cigars, or anything else for that matter, and have never read *The Financial Review*. All this does not make me sound that mature.

I have often said this to people in the past, and they have largely disagreed with my assessment. 'No…' they say, 'Nathan, you're very mature.'

I'm not so sure.

I was 29 when I went into Papua New Guinea with the Australian Army. The mission was known as Operation Bel Isi. In Tok Pisin, the local language, bel isi literally means that your stomach (bel) feels easy (isi). In the local tradition, if your stomach feels easy, life is good. So bel isi means good life. I reckon, overall, that's a great name for a military operation intended to bring stability and peace to a community.

I was there for about five months and our job was peace monitoring. There had been a horrible and painful civil war in Bougainville, in some ways fermented by the Australian mining interests working there at a huge copper mine. I don't believe there was ever a plan by these companies to push the people to civil war, but the poor management practices and apparent disregard for local frustrations certainly sealed the deal. By the time I got there, a ceasefire agreement was in place between the parties, and our mission was to monitor adherence to that agreement. In practice this meant visiting different villages and population centres, discussing life with the locals and asking if there had been any breaches of the agreement. There were different groups of soldiers doing the same job all over Bougainville and our area of operations was down in the south. We could see improvements in the lives of the villagers in our area. They were able to travel freely without being targeted by rival groups. They could sell produce in different regions. They could worship at local churches and hold family gatherings without the possibility of becoming a target of violence. These were real changes to the people's lives and important indicators of success for the mission.

The base I worked out of was just a collection of shacks and a small two-storey house in a clearing big enough for a helicopter to land on. About twelve of us lived there, if we were all in base, though this was rare. The base was called Buin, named after the small town nearby, which was a regional administrative centre for the government. All the staff here worked together fairly harmoniously. The way to do that is to make sure everyone gets his or her share of the hard work, and a corresponding amount, though usually not directly proportional, of free time.

We took it in turns to do rubbish collection and disposal. Not a fun job, at least you wouldn't think it was. In fact, in normal circumstances it would be one of my least favourite jobs. But, being stuck up in the middle of nowhere, you can make something out of nothing. They say, when you get a lemon, you make lemonade. When you're a commando and you get a lemon, you make explosions.

The person on duty on any particular day would collect all the food scraps and rubbish from the camp bins and bring them over to a large pit about 80 metres from the camp. He or she would (or should) then throw them in the pit, which was about 3 metres by 3 metres and about 2 metres deep. Then the person would (again, should) throw about a litre of diesel fuel on and around the rubbish, and ignite it. The resulting fire would make the rubbish in the pit a black mess that was totally unattractive to the local wildlife, or villagers for that matter. We were really trying to avoid any animals being attracted to our rubbish, because it would encourage a pest infestation. Of course, we didn't want the local villagers to start thinking about foraging through our rubbish either, as this could lead to accidents and associated problems. Once the fire had destroyed the rubbish to some degree, the person on duty would put a few shovelfuls of dirt on top. This way, it didn't stink, and, as environmentally unsound as it was, it wasn't really a bad system considering our circumstances. Every few months, when the pit was about three-quarters filled with rubbish, we would totally fill it in and dig a new pit.

Getting towards the end of my tour, things were, perhaps, a bit boring and we could see the light at the end of the 5-month-long tunnel. To us, that meant we were going home soon, and we were, therefore, a bit more excited every day. There was a friend of mine, Tim, on the team with me. He was a radio operator who had been attached to the commandos. He was a great guy, very intelligent and always looking for a challenge/mischief, whichever was more interesting.

It was Tim's turn to do the rubbish and I saw him walking over to the pit with a barrel full of refuse from the camp. I walked over to the pit and started talking to Tim. It didn't take too much encouragement for Tim to dump a fair bit more fuel than was necessary into the pit, just to add a bit of fun, and, if anyone asked, burn the rubbish more effectively. Tim was into it, and pretty soon the fire Tim would light that day promised to be the biggest rubbish-pit pyrotechnics display of the mission. I reckon there were about 5 to 10 litres of diesel in there. Nice. Tim had drawn the diesel fuel from large drums we kept on hand at our camp, and we also grabbed a litre of petrol, for good measure. The petrol helped the fire take a bit more easily than the diesel, while the diesel seemed to take longer to burn off, thoroughly burning our rubbish, and therefore better reducing it. That was our theory, anyway. Clearly, we were doing a great service to the mission by more aggressively reducing that rubbish. The more the fire reduced it, the longer it would be before we needed to dig a new rubbish pit. Really, we were doing a service for the soldiers who would follow us on this mission. And, we were going to make something go BANG, which was far more important.

Well, we stood back about 10 metres and Tim did the honours by throwing a burning rag into the pit. We crouched down and waited. Bingo. A very satisfying whuummp emanated from the pit. That's the sound you always hear when there's a diesel fuel explosion. It is indicative of the type of slow-speed detonation you get when burning unpressurised fuel. The actual explosion still feels quite voluminous as it disturbs a relatively large volume of the surrounding air, and a portion of that air presses against you and momentarily changes the air pressure close by. It is obviously totally different to the sharper, more violent crump noise you hear when a high explosive goes off, releasing its energy at an enormously faster rate. High explosive has a detonation speed of about 8 000 metres per second, so, when it goes off close by (and I can tell you that's an experience you should not necessarily seek), the overpressure shakes you, rocks your sense of balance, compresses your chest, makes your head hurt and generally disorientates you. They are mild effects, having no real lasting impact (we hope). Being closer still is obviously highly dangerous, even if we discount the possibility of being hit by flying debris.

Still, this was a good little explosion, reasonably satisfying, considering the circumstances. The temperature was about 30 – 35 degrees Celsius, so this had caused a fair amount of the fuel to turn into vapour and billow within the pit. When we looked at the pit, we saw a large conical orange flame extend out of the pit about 3 metres into the air. I suppose it was more of a flash, as it immediately disappeared from view.

'All clear,' Tim said and gave the thumbs-up. We were both smiling that cheeky, I-just-made-something-go-bang smile. Looking into the pit, we could see a nice little fire was blazing away, merrily burning the rubbish.

We were pretty happy with ourselves and the garbage was pretty much done. We both looked across the little track towards where the campsite commander's shack was…no reaction. We were in the clear. A few shovelfuls of dirt and we were on our way. No evidence, no witnesses, no worries.

Well, a few days later it was my turn to do the rubbish. I'm not too mature to indulge in a bit of one-upmanship so I decided to up the ante, and blow Tim's effort right out of the water, or rubbish pit.

I went around collecting rubbish in quite a fervour. I was throwing away anything that was not nailed down, and some things that were. Then, I would require a big fire to get rid of that big pile of rubbish, naturally. A big fire would require more than the usual amount of diesel, naturally. A big fire may create a big flame and loud noise on ignition, naturally.

So I filled the pit with my soon-to-be-flash-cooked rubbish. Anyway, when I had my pile together, I called Tim over. I must have looked like a mad scientist and he could tell, by the look on my face, that I was going to prosecute that rubbish with extreme prejudice.

Every good crime needs a good accomplice and Tim jumped straight in. I got about 30 litres of diesel and 15 litres of petrol. Timing was important, so that we had a good vapour cloud but did not start to lose too much fuel to evaporation. That was where the pit was perfect for these circumstances, trapping the vapour within its 2-metre walls. It was a hot wind-less day. Perfect again. The rubbish stayed sitting in the bright sunshine in the centre of the pit for about an hour before we started to properly prepare the fire.

We had three vehicles with us on the mission, and these were parked under a sort of carport inside the perimeter of the camp. The fuel was stored next to the carport in what we referred to as the fuel depot, but which was actually just a bunch of drums sitting on the ground and a couple of hand pumps. We walked back from the fuel depot with a trolley carrying the 'required' amounts of fuel. All good so far, as nobody had confronted us as to why we needed so much fuel.

We passed the base toilet, which was a tiny hut built over a long drop hole in the ground, constructed in the local style, with a toilet seat on top; very civilised. The hut was mainly built of bamboo and sac-sac leaves, which are like palm fronds, woven together to form a very lightweight, but not particularly robust, wall.

At the pit we prepared the ignition device. We knew this would be big when it went off and that we would need to be a reasonable distance away to be safe. So I got a good sized rock from the road nearby and tied a nice piece of rag to it. I put a little bit of fuel on the rag and laid it down at the site where we would start the fire. At the pit we carefully started pumping the diesel into the hole and tried to spread it all around the base of the pit, a 9 square metre area. I poured all the petrol into one concentrated area in the centre of the pit. Everything looked right, and nobody from the camp was nosing around. We were ready.

We gave it about five minutes. We used that time to get rid of the fuel drums, as these would be obvious evidence of our diabolical, but clearly enjoyable, plan. From our observation position about 20 metres away from the pit, you could see the hazy vapour cloud languidly rising from the hole. We crouched down to check that we could observe effectively and safely from that position. All good so far. The effect I was hoping for was going to be similar to a fuel/air bomb, which explodes, vaporising a quantity of fuel, then at an optimal point a fraction of a second later, has a secondary ignition which blows up the vapour in the air. The resultant explosion is very large. I was hoping to see this, on a very small scale.

I had to use heat to create my vapour but thought it would work on some level. I held the rock and cocked my arm back, ready to throw it at the pit. I had a last look around for witnesses. None. Time to pull the trigger. Tim lit the rag while it was in position with my arm cocked. I gave it a second for the little flame to really get going, then threw it.

We didn't have to wait long. We watched the rock/rag/ignition device gracefully arc through the air towards the pit. It was still well lit. But, while it was at least 5 metres from the pit, my monster came alive.

Oh my God! The flash was bright orange and seemed to reach right out to where Tim and I crouched, or at least had been crouching, as we were both now flat on our backs. Really, it was probably more of a natural reaction to the flame than the force of the flame knocking us over. Debris had been lifted from the pit and now flew through the air, apparently trying to break free from the bonds of gravity and take on a new life as some sort of rubbish-phoenix. The noise was awesome, deep and resonant, and a dirty black, but perfectly formed, mushroom cloud rose majestically into an otherwise cloudless sky. Oh yeah!

On the advice of my lawyers, I include the following very important information:

> This event was not fun in any way and was not exciting, wholly satisfying or interesting in any scientific sense. Also, boys—because let's face it, I'm speaking to boys here, girls will not, in any way, be attracted to these antics—attempting to replicate these events will most likely negatively affect your chances of hooking up with any cool girls for years to come.

I felt OK and assumed that Tim did as well. I knew we had to go into damage control right now. That was a LOUD bang, and would absolutely have got the attention of our commanders in the offices 80 metres away. If they looked out their windows and saw two soldiers lying on their backs and a mushroom cloud rising above their heads, we would be in serious trouble. However, if they looked out and saw two soldiers nonchalantly standing next to the pit, rakes in hand, watching rubbish burn, then our chances were better. Instinctively we both ran towards the pit to affect this calm and cool scene. It was damn hot near that pit, and a good little fire was burning, though a fair bit of the rubbish had been changed by the traumatic event that it had just endured.

I knew that I shouldn't even turn around to check if anyone was looking. Why would I? I didn't have anything to feel guilty about. Everything was perfectly normal, sir. Just another day at the garbage pit, sir. Nothing to see here, sir. Turning around and furtively looking over my shoulder would only make me seem like I had something to worry about.

After a while I snuck a peek over to the offices and saw the TSM, the senior-most soldier, watching proceedings from the top floor of the offices. He was a New Zealander, a great guy who ran a strict camp, and really would not approve of going nuclear in the garbage pit. I knew he wasn't sure what to do. We looked calm, but he was eyeing us suspiciously. He knew we had been up to something. Good instincts there, sir.

I looked back the other way and immediately knew we had some dramas. The rear wall of the toilet had been blown off and lay, otherwise intact, on the ground nearby. Hmmm?

We watched the fire for a while longer and I looked over my shoulder to see some of the local guys who lived nearby running up to see why the Australian base had exploded. Their panicked expressions were not going to help. I quickly told them everything was OK, downplaying the explosion, and asked if they could help repair the toilet. They had made it in the first place, so it would only take them a few minutes.

When we crossed back into camp I knew it was situation critical. It was all going to be about how we handled questions. Confidence is the key.

The TSM called me over and asked about the explosion. Can't be denied, better do some tap dancing here.

'Yes, sir, very loud. Gave Tim and I quite a shock. We used about eight litres of diesel and two litres of petrol, which was obviously too much. But, really, I think it was the fact that we left the fuel on the rubbish for too long before lighting it that caused the problem. It must have begun to evaporate and when it caught fire really made quite a bang. Did you see the mushroom cloud, sir? Looked like Hiroshima.'

He chuckled and said, 'Oh, I see. Well, you can't use that much fuel in the future. Yeah, no good letting it evaporate like that either. It could get dangerous.'

'Yep. No worries, sir. Oh, sir, when I went over to do the rubbish this morning I noticed the rear wall on the toilet was coming off. I asked one of the local guys to fix it a couple of hours ago, but I notice he's taken it off to do a proper job. He reckons it'll be done in an hour or so.'

'Oh, yeah? Good work.'

ICE-CREAM

I don't have a piece of paper proving that I am mature, but I do have one from the army proving I am sane. (It might have expired now though.)

I left that mission soon after. Tim and I rotated out at the same time, but all other staff were due to leave at different times, so there was some continuity to the mission. I had had a great time, really. It was a terrific mission to be part of because it was hugely successful and you could see improvements in the situation even in the small amount of time you were there. On this mission, the majority of the soldiers worked in a large base at a place called Loloho. It was relatively comfortable, having TV and movies, a gym, nice showers and a little shop. What the soldiers in there did not have was any real sense of the place and people and how beneficial their work actually was. I lived out at Buin so I would go on patrols for a few days at a time, staying in local villages, talking to people and hearing their concerns. We could see the effect our work had, and felt the true worth of the mission. Under those circumstances it is easy to work hard. In Loloho, I think it would be difficult to keep your spirits up, even with movies, ice-cream and a gym.

This being the case, before any soldiers leave the mission they are required to have a psychological debrief to make sure their mental health is OK. After having been home a few months they have another one. It's a good system, or at least an attempt to look after the mental health of soldiers, who sometimes have seen or been directly involved in traumatic events.

In our case at Buin, a psych doctor would fly down to conduct an interview to check your mental health. The interview usually takes about 45 minutes to an hour. If you have any issues they will hopefully be addressed or at least identified and you may not be sent on similar missions in the future.

When the psych doctor, who is a major, and therefore a relatively senior officer, arrives to do my interview, I'm not there. I'm returning from a patrol to a really remote part of our area of operations. When I return and get off the helicopter at the base, I stink like a goat and am covered in mud from a long hard climb through the jungle, which got us to the position where the helo picked us up.

I get off the chopper, dump my gear, and run over to where the major is waiting in an office which is just a spare shack.

I stick my head in the door and tell him that I will need a few minutes to shower and change into appropriate clothes for the interview, and he tells me there's no hurry and that I should take my time.

I have a nice refreshing shower and change into a sports uniform of shorts and T-shirt. As I walk out of the entrance of my accommodation I pass a large bright blue dress that is neatly folded on a seat. A lady who had been on the mission for a short time as a civilian observer had donated the dress for the girls in the local village. Ahhh, it hasn't got to them yet, but will, the next day. I can't resist. I whip off my T-shirt and slip the dress on over my shorts. Classic.

Tim walks in as I walk out. He knows I'm going to a psych interview.

'Do me up, Tim.'

He does, but he says just two words.

'Oh no.'

I march proudly straight to my interview.

I walk into the hut where the psych doctor is seated and betray no sense that anything is amiss.

'Good afternoon, sir. I am Lance Corporal Mullins. Sorry to have kept you waiting.'

He looks at me with an entirely blank expression. I sit down across the table from him. He is not laughing, as I had hoped he would be by now. He doesn't say a word. This is really one of those times when you get the feeling that a joke has gone over badly. He leans back in his chair and still doesn't speak. This is getting awkward now. I have to make a move.

'Sorry, sir. Just a bit of a joke. I don't wear dresses, ever. Well, this is the first time.' I stand up, this isn't going well, and I get the feeling that I'm going to pay a higher price than expected for this joke.

'Sir, I thought I would just lighten the mood a bit. Ahhh, I'm sure people often act crazy, as a joke, in interviews with you…'

He finally starts to crack a smile as he takes in the situation. He isn't exactly bursting out laughing, but I feel that I, at least, will not be detained and hospitalised. That is a good thing.

'No one has ever, ever, acted crazy in an interview with me. I suppose most people are too stressed about making a good impression during the interview to act like they're crazy.'

I can tell by the inflection he uses when he says the word crazy that he isn't comfortable saying it, but has only used the term because I had used it. He is lightening up though, so I am happier.

'I'll go and put a T-shirt on if you can wait just a moment, sir.'

I rush away and put my T-shirt back on. When I return to the shack everything is OK. The major is shaking his head and giggling to himself.

We talk about my last few months on Operation Bel Isi and after about fifteen minutes that is it. I say it was a pretty short interview and he agrees. He says, 'Nathan, if you're comfortable enough to walk into an important interview like this, wearing a dress just to make a joke, then I have no fear about your mental health and would say you're pretty well adjusted.'

So, there it is. If you want to convince a psych doctor that you're sane, wear a dress like you're crazy. Oh, ladies, I don't know what you should do, sorry.

If blowing up rubbish and wearing dresses in psych interviews isn't immature, then I'm about to put the last nail in the coffin. Oh well, we both knew what we were getting into with this book.

One-upmanship is hard to resist. There was this guy on the mission with us, a New Zealand Maori named Ehaka. Now he was a pretty tough guy, and good to work with, but we seemed, at times, to have a sort of rivalry.

Once we went on a patrol to a remote coastal village on the south coast of the island of Bougainville. The village is called Tokuaka, and is quite difficult to access, as no roads take you to the village, and the foot trail in is quite rough and hard to navigate. We got down there by landing craft, a large flat-bottomed boat with a flop-down front ramp, so you could drive vehicles on and off. We were due to hang around for a few days then clear a landing zone in the jungle somewhere and get a helicopter to pick us up.

When we got to the village, it was totally deserted, but rather eerily had obviously been recently inhabited. If it had been a Hollywood movie you would have got the hell out of there right away, as it was sure to be the scene of some sort of horror, but in the real world it turns out that everyone in the village had gone to a religious festival, and no evil forces were at work.

The village was right on the beach, with a swampy narrow lake or lagoon running behind most of the village on the land side. It was a beautiful site and all the huts were built high on stilts. I had a good look around the water and surrounding land and could not really see how it would flood, so I was perplexed as to why the houses were on stilts. That night we worked it out. The patrol members slept on the ground in the centre of the village. Except for me, as I always slept in a hammock in the tropics and couldn't believe that everyone else didn't, because hammocks are really cool and comfortable in that environment.

There was no flood but we woke to find crocodile tracks all around the outside of the village, some of them made by huge crocs. I saw a medium-sized crocodile about 200 metres down the beach that morning and watched it languidly climb up the beach from the ocean and slink into the swamp. When we looked in the huts, each one had a 4-metre-long, sharpened pole, obviously to fend off nosey crocs. These weren't really fashioned into spears, but were very sharp and heavy enough to do the job.

Pretty soon Ehaka and I started to talk about previous hunting experiences and the one-upmanship was flying. Almost as a dare I suggested we each take a pole and try to spear a crocodile in the swamp. The truth was I was hoping he wouldn't want to do it, because then I wouldn't have to do it either. Ahh, no. Apparently, he was just as stupid as I was. I have never wanted to spear a crocodile before or since and can't think why we wanted to then.

Anyway, an hour later we were walking in ankle-deep water in the swamp, looking for crocodiles to spear. When I type these words now, I feel ridiculous. We each had one of those long heavy poles up on our shoulders and had the amazingly optimistic idea that we would launch the spears at some unsuspecting crocs and spear them to death. Then, we would return to camp, likely wearing a crocodile head as a hat like some prehistoric hunters, once and for all proving our manhood. Great idea, boys.

We walked through the swamp for about an hour and had seen nothing. Those poles were getting heavy. When we looked down at our feet we could see that we had gradually, insidiously, strayed into deeper water. The water was now above our knees, but the mud bottom was not too sticky and unstable yet.

A while later and we could see a good size croc on the other side of the swamp about 200 metres away, sitting on the bank, half out of the water. After a second he or she slipped into the water and swam away, further inland, away from us. Croc hunting was taking a lot of time, especially when carrying a heavy pole, but it seemed that we were finally getting into proper croc territory. The sight of that croc had emboldened, or, in fact, en-stupided, us. We were about 10 metres apart, each hoping to be the first to bag one. Though, I don't really know where you could get a bag big enough to put a crocodile in. We walked towards the area where the croc had been and again did not consciously take in the change in water level.

Looking down I realised I was waist-deep in water. I looked over at Ehaka, and he didn't seem disconcerted, so, neither was I. Damn it!

We both saw the croc at the same time. He was making a broad but low bow wave as he swam. He looked big, and was slowly swimming towards us from about 100 metres away. This was it. At last. His body seemed to be hardly moving. Just sort of drifting towards us. Only a slight flicker of movement betrayed that he was not a log. He was easy to see and track. Even though he was still well out of spear range, I had my arm cocked and ready to spear him. Everything was looking good for a Nathan/Ehaka victory over the crocodiles. No worries. Well, maybe some little ones, I suppose.

At 50 metres it happened. Somehow, we had never anticipated the following eventuality. The croc picked up his pace towards us just a bit then dropped from sight altogether. He disappeared immediately and completely. The situation was suddenly crystal clear to me and I couldn't believe that it had not been clear to me earlier.

He was an enormously powerful and magnificently designed apex predator, the king of his swampy domain, which he knew like the back of his hand (if he had one). His dominance was totally unchallenged by any other animal. He moved with the stealth, unseen power and coiled potential of an attack submarine.

I, on the other hand, was a soft, small, unstable meal of tasty red meat, carrying a highly ineffectual weapon that I had never even seen before today. I moved with the speed and grace of a crayfish covered in toffee trying to climb a set of marble stairs. I was waist-deep in water and mud, and head-deep in trouble.

I looked at Ehaka and he had obviously made the same assessment. Without a word we turned and ran, well, sloshed, I suppose, towards the shore, too far away, at 100 metres. My heart was beating like a timpani drum. After we got about 10 metres up the bank we stopped and looked at each other. We didn't need to say anything. Idiots, just plain idiots. I don't think we engaged in much one-upmanship after that. It cured me for a while, that's for sure. It was a long, introspective walk back to the camp.

Back at the camp one of the guys asked me how we went.

'Oh, fine. Didn't see anything, though.'

> **My overworked legal team has advised me to include a warning here. Hunting crocodiles is illegal in most places, and won't win you any friends anyway. Hunting crocodiles by creeping around in a swamp, 'armed' with a spear is stupid and highly ineffective. Don't do it.**

We could only communicate with hand gestures, but I was pretty sure this Pakistani soldier wanted to be in a photo with me. Or he wanted to marry me. I took the photo option.

The helo arriving was a momentous and amazing spectacle for these people, probably akin to the space shuttle, piloted by the your favourite movie star, landing in the main street of your town. Problem was the huge drop on the other side of the landing zone.

CHAPTER 7

Laugh, and the whole world laughs with you, but then crying will make you look sensitive to women

Osama Bin Laden, a Catholic priest and a horse walk into a pub…

In adversity, maintain your sense of humour. The harder the situation, the more important this will become. I don't mean that you need to become flippant or be some sort of buffoon; you still need to make a good assessment of what is going on and some grounded decisions. However, it is healthy sometimes to regard circumstances that conspire against you with a level of petulance or virtual disrespect. Disrespect to the point that you make jokes about the situation, however life-threatening it may seem. This may seem ridiculous, but everything seems a little bit clearer and a little bit less shocking when we can crack a joke about it.

I recall paddling in two-man collapsible sea kayaks in the Yarra River in Melbourne. We were on an army exercise and paddling these blacked-out kayaks, called Kleppers, around the shipping channels. The Kleppers consist of a folding wooden frame that gets inserted into a rubberised canvas outer layer. You sit one behind the other on little seats, and hope your teamwork is up to scratch and you don't paddle around in circles arguing. They teach good seamanship, and reliance on a partner, but the main lesson they teach is how wonderful a nice noisy, smelly outboard motor attached to a little boat can be. Kleppers are very useful for moving around estuarine environments and are even stable and sturdy enough for the open ocean. In fact, people have crossed the Pacific and Atlantic oceans in them, solo. When you get to land you can break them down to hide them, bury or sink them, or just fold them up and carry them with you. In Europe, people take them on trains for holidays and paddle across lakes they stop at on the way. (Personally, I would prefer to be in a sleeper carriage, to be gently awoken by the steward, and whisked away to the waiting luxury motor cruiser that will take me over the lake.)

On the night in question there were three Kleppers and therefore six crewmen, one pair in each boat. We had been paddling for a couple of hours, practising our teamwork and paddling technique and making sure we were well versed in the general operation and handling of the craft. We had crossed the shipping channel quite close to the broad mouth of the Yarra River at dusk, in front of a large container ship that was making its way into Port Phillip Bay from the dock area further up the river. The ship was huge, and seemed even more massive relative to our tiny human-powered boats. Moving among these giants was always risky and took excellent coordination by each pair. But ill-timing had put us way too close to the ship and dangerously close to being swept under the giant's bows. We sprinted across its bow and (hopefully) out of the way and turned the boats to face the ship. This tactic allowed the boats to have the best chance of riding out the powerful bow wave that was fast approaching. Being hit abeam, or from a diagonal or perpendicular angle, would be likely to flip our craft. Nobody wanted to be suddenly bobbing around in an upturned craft as the ship steamed by, way too close. These container ships suck water towards their stern and propellers, and if we had been capsized and thrown into the water there was a chance we would be swept along and into that messy end. Being sucked under the huge ship would, well, suck. This was a situation I was keen to avoid, and I'm sure I wasn't alone on that idea.

We were close to the other Kleppers and my partner and I braced our paddles in the water. It was touch and go. I heard one of the guys nervously describe the ship. He probably couldn't think of anything else to say in this stressful moment, but wanted to say something to break the mood.

'It's Russian.'

We all looked up to where the ship's name was painted on the bow. You could see that the guy who called out had mistaken the Greek lettering conventions for the similar-looking Russian Cyrillic style of lettering.

I yelled back, 'Nah. It's Greek.'

By then he had recognised his own mistake. After a second of silence he said, 'I meant it's going fast. You know? Rushin'…'

We all burst out laughing as the bow wave hit us and bounced us violently against each other. We couldn't stop laughing, and, I suppose, we didn't want to stop until we were safe again.

In late 2006 I began working in Iraq. I went there as a police trainer for the Iraqi National Police. It was an interesting and, at times, exciting job. For the most part I lived out in the middle of the desert, at a place called An Numaniyah. It was an Iraqi army base, and a section of it had been given over for the training of Iraqi police officers. Being a police officer in Iraq is a dangerous job, as the militant enemy targets them for attacks. At recruiting and training centres all over the country there had been terrible attacks, costing many lives. That was why our training camp was centred in an Iraqi army base, in a remote desert area. It certainly wasn't to take advantage of the abundant dust storms, flat featureless terrain, camel spiders or extreme heat.

While I was there an Australian mate of mine, Pat, got shot. This is not as common as you might imagine. The circumstances in this case were even more uncommon, because Pat had shot himself, accidentally. Now, Pat was a great guy. He was smart, easy-going and very professional. He had a great sense of humour too, thank goodness.

Pat had been practising pistol shooting on the shooting range one day, and, while he was putting his pistol back in his holster, he shot himself in the leg. As a medic I know a fair bit about this. When you get shot in the leg there are many possible implications and permutations of the injury and actions of the bullet. Everything depends on the path the bullet takes, and therefore how and where the bullet imparts its energy to the body being struck. You could easily lose your leg because of such an injury, and the damage to arteries in the upper leg, from gunshots can be enormous. This could prove to be a highly serious situation.

I was nearby and heard what had happened on the radio so I made my way over as fast as possible. Pat was lying down at the firing point on our shooting range and there was a small pool of blood on the ground. The fact that it was a small pool was a good start, but was inconclusive as evidence that he did not have a serious bleed, as the blood could have been pooling somewhere out of sight. The other guys who were with him when he shot himself had exposed Pat's leg. When I assess casualties I always look at their faces, obviously at their wounds as well, but a look in their face is a good start. You can quickly tell if they can breathe, if they're in pain, starved of oxygen, etc. This is especially useful if you know the person well. If you know how a person looks ordinarily, then a glance at their face can tell you a lot about their condition. Pat's face told me a great deal. He was not fighting for his life; he was smiling and seemed pretty happy, all things considered. I mean, I'm sure he had happier times than this, but, well, you know what I mean. The first words that came out of my mouth were, 'What have you done here, Lefty?'

Instant nickname. Merciless, and appropriate at the same time. (They're the best kind of nicknames. I once knew a really ugly man nicknamed The Sun. He was called that because if you looked at him too long, your eyes hurt! That's right, merciless and appropriate.) The attendant guys standing around instantly came down a level of terror. Everyone became more confident and relaxed and, in a real critical incident, this has a correspondingly positive influence on team efficiency and individual decision-making.

Pat was the perfect patient. He was in pain, but laughing, cracking jokes and quite at ease with the situation, again, all things considered. I have known grown men who have stubbed their toes and reacted with more horror and required more reassurance than Pat after he had been shot. The bullet had entered Pat's leg on the upper right of the outside of his thigh, tracked down about 20 centimetres then punched out of his leg and down into the ground. It didn't hit any bone on the way through and hadn't damaged any arteries or veins. A bullet brings a pressure wave on its path through the body, and this pressure wave usually does a great deal of damage to tissue that has a hard time quickly expanding to accommodate the pressure wave. In Pat's case the bullet tracked just under the skin, and the pressure wave really didn't interact with much tissue that couldn't expand quickly. He was very lucky. As a medic I was very happy that this was a simple injury, with no broken bone etc., and that Lefty was a fit, strong patient, who was taking this in his stride. Well, obviously not literally.

Lefty looked at me and asked, 'Will I be able to play lacrosse?'

'Yeah, mate. Of course.'

Then he said, 'Good, because I couldn't before.'

Needless to say, we patched Lefty up and the US military were even kind enough to CASEVAC him to Baghdad for further treatment. While we were waiting for the helo, he pulled out his mobile phone and asked me to ring his wife and tell her the news.

SILENCE

Now, as you can imagine, news like this has to be handled delicately. You are always pretty careful informing loved ones that their partner in Iraq is, well, anything really, because they're expecting the worst and you don't want to scare them if it's unnecessary.

Lefty handed me his phone and I dialled his wife, who I had never spoken to in my life.

'Hi, Fiona. This is Nathan Mullins. You don't know me but I work with Pat. Don't worry. Everything is alright. Pat's fine, but…he has been shot. But really, only a little bit shot, and he did it himself, so, you know, that's good.'

Silence.

After a few seconds Fiona fully comprehended what I had said and we had a longer conversation about the events and what would happen next. I would say that she took the news with the sort of good humour and practical commonsense that is decidedly uncommon. She was great. Either that, or she in fact hated Pat and the news that he had shot himself was great.

Lefty got better very soon. He was running again within a couple of weeks after having decided to go Dirty Harry on his own leg. Overall, he healed up very well. Oh well, the real price he paid for shooting himself is people, justifiably, making jokes at his expense for the rest of his life. Now it's immortalised in print, too.

MISSION ESSENTIAL

I was on an army exercise years ago in a large bush training area in Victoria. Now, some army exercises are meant to test and/or practise your abilities in the full range of skills you require to carry out the job of a soldier. At some point you will navigate, using map, compass and GPS, and at another time you will have a complex tactical problem to solve; perhaps you will need to stealthily approach a target and quietly take over a position, or create a loud distraction and then prosecute your attack. You may have begun the exercise by parachuting into the exercise area or you may have driven small inflatable boats a long distance to get there. It may be that during the exercise you are confronted with a large cliff to scale. In every exercise there are challenges to your fitness and your ability to recall what you have previously been taught.

Then there are overexercises. Purely designed to wear you down and test your physical toughness. Not really your fitness, just your doggedness. These are long, arduous, tough, physical efforts that may go on for days without any respite. You may be carrying a pack of between 30 and 40 kilograms and you may not even take that pack off for the entire course of the exercise. You have your head down and just keep moving.

During an ordeal like this you need two things. At the top of the list is a good sense of humour, and next is a good, logical, practical way of packing. Your pack needs to be carefully packed and repacked to make sure everything fits comfortably. Everything must be in the perfect place and ordered in a logical, easy-to-understand way. Nothing superfluous was added and you would get rid of weight in every practical way. This is so you had room for Mission Essential Items: bullets and bombs, med kit, radios, spare batteries, cold weather gear, climbing equipment, observation equipment, etc. You carried a notebook (always) that had only enough pages in it to last the duration of the exercise. You cut your pencil down so it was a small, but still useable, nub. You took the handle off your metal cup and got the lightest cooking utensils possible. Many guys had titanium cutlery. When I say cutlery, I mean one spoon; to carry more than a spoon was ridiculous. In a temperate climate, if it rained you got wet—'Harden up, Princess' was what you used instead of a raincoat, though I never found those sorts of phrases particularly helpful.

On the subject of phrases, another one that got bandied about when the going got tough was, 'Pain is just weakness leaving the body.'

Thanks, Einstein. You must be very proud.

Another ripper, that clearly made me feel better about the situation, was, 'Don't wish for a lighter pack, wish for a stronger back.'

Yeah, sure. That will fix everything.

I remember a particularly ridiculous one that I used to use as an instructor, when I could identify troops trying to walk up steep hills during special forces selection events: 'Lean into the hill, and let the hill work for you.'

I only used that to annoy people, not because I thought it was particularly rousing. I remember my own instructors saying it to me, and thinking, 'Are you kidding, you idiot? Do you know ANY physics? How would that help?' I reckon, just like me, they were kidding. Just trying to exacerbate people and get them to quit.

HIGH-ENERGY MEALS

So, anyway, we travelled as light as we could. Usually, we carried no comfort items at all. No sleeping mat or pad to use as a chair or mattress. Nothing. You probably wouldn't sleep anyway. People believe we bring books or magazines, radios and CD players, etc. Rubbish. Only military kit was in our packs. Everyone's pack was the same. It didn't matter whether you were in charge of the patrol or the whole unit, your pack was full to the brim with the gear you would need for fighting, and nothing else.

It was in the midst of doing one of these exercises, nearly two days in, when I literally had not removed my pack and was feeling pretty low, that we stopped to eat a meal. You have to eat, no two ways about it. If you don't eat, and you burn calories like we did, then you fall over and don't get up. If you can't get up, you can't complete your mission. That just isn't allowed. So we carried dehydrated, high-energy meals. They didn't taste that good, but were light and gave the sustenance you required. There were no heavy cans or glass, everything was in plastic packaging so you could fold it back up and stow it in your pack.

On this particular patrol there were six of us and I was second scout, walking along behind (logically) the first scout. Behind me was the guy in charge, John. He was navigating us through a large, rocky, undulating bush training area in central Victoria. John was a very experienced corporal. Always calm and authoritative. He signalled me to harbour up, which means stop and go into a defensive posture for a rest, or meal, or to speak on the radio, or check our position accurately. The scouts would basically face the direction we had come from and everyone else would form a circle with the scouts' position being the 12 o'clock. Easy done.

After a minute or so everyone was in position. We all waited quietly, giving the bush around us time to get used to us and, theoretically, waiting to see if anyone had been following us. Nope, nobody following, so all good then. Silence was golden for us. As six guys we were not looking for a fight, we were looking to move quietly and without an obvious impact until we could meet up with the rest of the force and get up to some proper mischief. Six guys can't put up a sustained resistance and we had no vehicle to move around in, so running from the enemy was our only practical option, and that's a very poor option, at best. Therefore, our plan was not to run into anyone while we were in such a small group, and try to be as sneaky as we could. We would not have said more than a handful of words in the last two days, and those would have been whispered. The rest of the time we communicated by hand signals.

Anyway, we were all in position, facing out, listening and watching. John gave the signal for us to eat. I looked at the number-one scout and signalled him to eat first. We would take it in turns.

I was buggered and was pretty happy to get the chance to remove my heavy pack. The first scout was eating away and would be finished soon. I took a glance over at John, to see if he needed to pass on any messages, and was astounded. I was very close to bursting out laughing.

John had taken off his pack, like me, for the first time since the exercise began, opened the top flap and was removing an entire, huge pineapple, complete with the spiky fronds on top.

PINEAPPLE

Unbelievable. There must have been many times in the last two days when John would have hated that pineapple and the extra 2 kilos it added to his pack. Even if your pack is ultra-comfortable when you start an exercise like this, after a day or two of constant wearing, it feels like somebody has replaced your pack with a refrigerator, and attached it to your shoulders with barbed wire. I couldn't believe that John had carried such an incongruous item. It looked and felt so out of place that I couldn't really comprehend it. Hilarious. John smirked at me and nodded. In lieu of laughter, I just shook my head. By now everyone else had looked in and done the same. It was a classic moment, and John must have been looking forward to breaking that pineapple out the whole way through the patrol.

We all got a piece, actually, several, and it was easily the sweetest pineapple I have ever had.

Morale was high.

There is a trick to this maintain-your-sense-of-humour-through-adversity stuff. That is, it is one thing to keep a good sense of humour and high spirits while circumstances conspire to make your life miserable, it is another to observe something bad happening to somebody else and then be amused. I can tell you that, in this situation, the person who is miserable some-times does not subscribe to the humour-in-adversity thing.

When I was nineteen years old, a few friends and I spent a lot of time surfing. We were all working or studying at the time, but any spare couple of hours we had, we would flash away down the coast and have a surf. Life was good.

My friend Craig had an early '80s model Toyota Cressida station wagon that was bright red in colour. Not fast or sexy, but entirely serviceable and handy for carrying a car full of surfboards and surfers.

It was hot, around 35 degrees Celsius, and we were going for a surf outside a nice small town called Anglesea, in Victoria. To get to the surf spot we had to drive down about 5 kilometres of seldom-used dirt road. Once we turned off the main highway onto the dirt road, we had developed the habit of sitting out on the bonnet and roof of Craig's car while he drove along the dirt track. (I think you probably already know where this is going.)

This particular day I sat on the roof, above the driver's side, with one foot dangling down onto the windscreen and one foot on the driver's windowsill. I felt pretty secure up there. Well, I felt secure as long as we kept the speed pretty low, as there was really nothing to hold on to. Our friend John (a different John from the shark story) sat on the other side, in a similar position, over the front seat passenger, which was Pete. It couldn't have been easy for Craig to drive the car with legs all over the windscreen and in the side windows. Tough luck. It wasn't all beer and skittles up on the roof either.

It was a windy road and, despite the recent heat, there were a few large deep puddles along the way, which provided some excitement as Craig sloshed the car through them. You got pretty splattered with water, but who cared? In ten minutes you would be in the cool salty waters of the Southern Ocean, enjoying a few waves. I was dressed in the boardshorts that I would wear in the water and I had a singlet on. I was wearing runners too. The only piece of clothing John wore was his trusty pair of boardshorts. No shoes, no shirt, nothing else.

Pretty soon we were laughing, having been pretty much drenched with filthy brown water from a deep puddle. The track was in reasonably good condition, other than the puddles. The local shire, as was and is common, used a coarse aggregate of yellowy stones to pave the road. This type of surface was always really rough to walk on in bare feet as many rocks were sharp and they varied in size from very small to the size of a mandarin. In the centre of the track there was always a raised ridge, generally consisting of larger stones, and these large stones also collected along the edges of the road, but in the actual wheel tracks, the stones were usually much smaller.

I have been advised by my ever-growing legal team to make a statement here.

Riding on the roof of a motor vehicle, or in any other manner except that intended by the manufacturer, is not fun. Especially not the roof, on dirt tracks, in summer, on your way to a surf beach.

Surviving such a ride will not grant you legend status among your mates, or in any way enhance your reputation with the ladies.

Again, I'm pretty obviously talking to the guys here.

RIGHTHANDER

A few turns came up on the track, we had about 2 kilometres to drive before we got to the water, and Craig was pushing on the speed a bit. We slid around one corner and it was getting a bit exciting trying to stay on the roof. No worries though, I thought. The next series of bends came up and the first slide was a lefthander, favouring John being able to stay on the car, as his weight was thrown towards the centre of the vehicle, where he could plant his hand on the roof as it slid through the turn. I stayed put—just—giggled and was thankful for having survived the turn. I looked over to see John grinning like a lunatic. He immediately banged on the roof of the car and yelled, 'Come on, Craig. Faster!'

Craig didn't need much encouragement. We approached the next corner, a righthander, a fair bit quicker and, judging by Craig's car placement on the approach, he intended to slide through this one, just like the last. Of course, this time the righthand corner favoured my side of the rooftop passenger position, as I would be forced towards the centre of the car as we went around.

John was still crazy-eyed and let out a yell.

I looked across as we entered the corner and I could immediately see that John was not going to be here for the whole trip. A look of terror gripped him and he seemed to slowly slide off the roof, with nothing to impede his fast-approaching meeting with the gravel road and mandarin-sized yellow rocks. He slid off and was gone. I watched as he valiantly, or maybe pathetically, tried to run it out. Unfortunately for John, who was a fast runner, not even an Olympic finalist could have ever done such a feat. He probably took about two steps, at 50 kilometres per hour, before going down. He disappeared from my view, and, amid screaming and much banging on the roof, Craig pulled up. The stop was too fast for me and I was rocketed forward, bouncing on the bonnet but landing on my feet on the track. I sprinted back to John, quickly joined by Pete.

John was balled up on the track. Blood seeped from head-to-toe rashes and gouges. Predictably, his boardshorts had not exactly provided top-notch crash protection to John's, now bloodied, body. File that away: shorts = poor protection. Between the mud and blood he looked like a wild animal that had been run over by some stampeding herd of buffalo. But he was OK. No broken bones or serious injuries. Pete and I made this same assessment at the exact same moment, as Craig ran up to us, shaken by the trampled and bloodied look of John. I looked at Pete and we could not contain ourselves. We burst out laughing and couldn't stop. In a few seconds we had to hide ourselves in some nearby bushes, hoping beyond hope to stop offending John with our laughter and to remove ourselves from his current glare and spitting insults. I couldn't blame him. But, after all, he was OK, and maybe it was the diametric change from believing your mate would be near death, to 'that was a Funniest Home Video moment' that got us. Either way we couldn't control the laughter. Tears streamed down my face and I tried to physically hold my mouth shut with one hand. John continued to glare at us and was clearly disgusted at our lack of sympathy. Craig, at least, was able to help him up and back to the car. John blamed Craig for the whole thing, in its entirety, though we tried to remind him of banging on the roof and yelling for more speed. For the rest of the day, I couldn't look John in the face without laughing.

It took John years to forgive Craig, if he ever really did.

Anyway, I can pretty much guarantee that John does not really subscribe to the crack-a-few-jokes-while-you-feel-bad-and-that-way-you-feel-better theory, and in fact probably subscribes to the those-bastards-couldn't-stop-laughing-at-me theory. It was the good-natured laugh you have about a close friend. I'm sure that if Pete and I had been confronted with a stranger who had met the same fate as John that day, we would not have laughed. But when it's your mate, and he's not seriously injured after such a dramatic (and hilarious) fall, you're allowed a laugh, or two. Hey, maybe John's right. I would just caution readers to choose carefully.

Good luck with that. I have no hope of containing myself in these situations.

CHAPTER 8

Practise critical observation

'Now pay attention class, this is important.'

When a teacher or instructor of some type says this, you better wake up. That means it is going to be in the test. He or she is trying to hint that whatever they will say next is going to be in the exam. Great, and I always appreciate that sort of assistance to my cause. I actually do enjoy learning new things anyway, so I am usually able to pay attention longer than most. I'm lucky like that. The subject barely even matters to me, learning some new information is exciting. I once spent an interesting week learning about light spectrums and laser properties for a course in the army, and frequently looked around the room to find everyone else asleep. I thought there was something wrong with me (there still may be) because I was interested. After all, these were my peers.

That is not the only time you need to pay attention though. You need to have a critical look at your surrounds, and make a quick analysis, constantly. Usually our structured life allows us to breeze through making a few left or right turns here and there, but always basically following a nice, predetermined, well-trodden course. Nothing wrong with that, and, in fact, that's what humanity has been trying to achieve since we crawled out of the primordial swamp, those of us that have, that is.

But, when you throw a few course corrections in, and give the well-trodden path the swerve, you need to take a bit more responsibility for yourself. This applies to anyone who undertakes endeavours that routinely risk their lives to a greater degree than the rest of us. I refer here to people like alpinists or skydivers, or people who are routinely exposed to critical incidents, like emergency services workers, or people who travel or live outside their own cultural settings, off the normal tourist routes. These people need to pay attention, just like the teacher says. Things go from reasonably peaceful to 'Oh shit' really quickly in these circumstances, and you need to be watching what is going on.

In 1998 I was doing a military exchange with soldiers from the Special Boat Squadron of the Bruneian Army. In Brunei the host unit would show us around their facilities and do a number of training exercises with us.

In Australia we have pretty high safety standards in both civil society and in the military. It is rare for us to have soldiers killed during training accidents, and when it does unfortunately happen, there are huge ramifications and enquiries. We are precious about our soldiers because it reflects the values of our society. In Australia we place a very high value on human life. Surprisingly, this isn't the case in many other countries. In many South-East Asian countries I could name, there is little institutional care for either the general population, or those in government employment, like soldiers. Soldiers are more like commodities in these places, and seem to be expended at alarming rates, even in peacetime.

In Brunei it's not too bad, but they certainly don't demand the high safety standards that soldiers in Australia adhere to. So, when you go overseas on exchange you get let off the leash to some degree, and can make training more realistic. Of course, with that extra realism comes extra liability, and an accompanying degree of extra attention and responsibility is required of every individual.

I once took part in a range practice where we shot 40-mm grenades from a grenade launcher attached to the underside of our rifles, out over a wide field littered with car bodies and old drums that we used as targets. Before we started firing we approached the firing point through these targets to inspect them. The idea was to look at them before and after firing at them, to see the weapons' effects. It is always good to have a clear idea about how effective your weapons are.

Well, we start firing the grenades that the Bruneians supply us with, and about one in five do not detonate. They have supplied the twenty of us with about 200 grenades, which is a pretty good number. I loved firing 40-mm rounds because they only travel at about 200 metres a second, so you can see them flying through the air in their arc towards their target. Then when they get there, even better, they explode. Who wouldn't enjoy that? Anyway, I had never before or since seen a high explosive 40-mm grenade not detonate, so this is unusual. It does happen in Australia, but it is relatively rare. If one does not detonate in Australia, it is likely you will stop the practice and get a specialist to find the unexploded ordnance and blow it up in a controlled detonation.

Over here they don't care, and our liaison officer just smiles and tells us not to worry about it. Of course, we are littering the area with unexploded ordnance, that may or may not explode the next time somebody walks through to inspect the targets. The senior Australian soldier who is present, a very experienced guy with many years in the special forces community, calls a stop. He isn't happy to have the soldiers in his charge create a massive area that is critically dangerous, regardless of what country it is in.

That range is exactly the area we had walked across 30 minutes before, and I'm sure this is not the first time that their rounds had proved to be unreliable.

Arriving in a country with safety standards like that, it should have occurred to me that their grenade range would be littered with bombs just waiting to blow up and tear my legs off, but it didn't. I had applied our standards to the situation, and did not pay attention to the full circumstances.

You can bet, when we left the range, we did not wander out through the firing range, blithely inspecting targets as we left. I was quite happy to just assume they made good holes in the cars.

A few days later we were at another range, this time to carry out a pit-clearing exercise. The idea is that the range emulates a set of fighting pits that are occupied by an imaginary enemy. These pits are rectangular holes in the ground, somewhat ironically resembling graves, from which soldiers defend their positions when they are under attack. Each pit has another about 20 metres behind it so the defence is layered. On this range the pits continue like this in a line for about 100 metres. There are cardboard cut-out targets in the pits, and the real soldiers emulate the attackers, not the defenders in the pits.

Two Bruneian soldiers are going to give us a demonstration of clearing the pits of any enemy. These guys are always energetic, so this will be great.

We stand in a group about 5 metres from the first pit, with the two Bruneian soldiers. Suddenly one of them drops to a knee, lets out a bloodcurdling scream and starts firing at the first target. My fingers go straight in my ears. Despite my police and military careers, I hate loud noises. His partner begins to crawl forward then turns to us with a silly look on his face. He pulls a grenade out, pulls the pin, and allows the handle to bounce off, thereby starting the 4–6 second (nobody is really sure) fuse.

After a few seconds he calmly drops the grenade into the pit, 5 metres from where I stand. I look across at the guy next to me and say, 'Do you reckon that was a live grenade?'

CRUMP! No need to answer. The first row of guys, me included, is knocked over, and everyone is splattered with mud, has ringing ears and a sore head. The Bruneians carry on.

I should have paid attention, or just stood at the back. Never mind, I know now.

Each pit has a small target at the front to represent an enemy soldier to shoot at. The Bruneian pair take turns to take out the pits, one man crawling up, while the other shoots at the target to suppress the enemy's reaction to attack. When the crawling man gets to the pit, he throws a grenade in and waits a few seconds while it turns the fictitious enemy in the pit into a fictitious blood and bone milkshake.

This is a dangerous drill which requires you to shoot just past your mate as he approaches the pit. Your mate has to take out a grenade, pull the pin, release the handle, wait a couple of seconds, allowing the grenade to 'cook off', then calmly drop it into the pit. This is so nobody in the pit has enough time to pick up the grenade and throw it out. You can see that there are plenty of ways for this to go wrong. We all know about the poor quality of explosive equipment they use. One in five 40-mm grenades did not go off; I wonder how carefully the fuse timing on these grenades was checked.

Usually, we would do that sort of drill without bullets and bombs first, then progress to bullets only, then bullets and grenades to top it off. This way everyone gets used to how it looks and feels and there is a much smaller chance of accident. Not in Brunei though.

Next time I decided to pay attention from the rear of the group, and let somebody else see up close.

In Iraq I pretty much took it for granted that I had to pay attention. Everybody was assumed to be a big boy over there, so along with that came a necessary level of taking personal responsibility.

I would work for eight weeks straight, then had four weeks off. I had to fly in and out of Baghdad International

Air Port—BIAP, which was always said as a word not spelled out like an acronym. It is important for Iraq to keep BIAP open for business, so Iraqi and foreign businesspeople and staff for the hundreds of civilian contracts can come and go. To that end it has about four large US military bases around the outside. These bases run their own operations in support of the wider Baghdad and Iraq theatre, but also bolster the security of the airport. The airport itself is secured, internally, if you will, by a large private security company. BIAP is a very attractive target and has been attacked many times, in all manner of ways. As it stands, it is pretty hard to attack the airport in a really effective way. It is just too large and too well surrounded by coalition forces. But, where there is a will, there is a way. In Iraq, there is a will.

At this exact time, I personally was very happy. That was because I was on my way home to Australia for a month's leave and had travelled the dangerous trip from the base where I worked in southern Iraq, first to the secure Green Zone, then along a particularly hazardous stretch of road to BIAP. We had made it without incident and that was a great start. Each step you made along that road was a little bit safer, and I was one hour away from stepping onto the plane which would take me on the short trip to Dubai.

Dubai was so incongruous with the situation in Iraq that some people found it hard to adjust to. It is an ultra-indulgent and lavishly appointed retail mecca. More importantly, arriving there was, symbolically at least, going home. While you were still in Iraq anything could happen. Delays were common and staying in Iraq longer than you had to was hard to take. Once you were in Dubai, you were on easy street, and just had to get to the beautiful airport for the flight home.

I was with a group of eight guys. All were ex-military or policemen from Australia or the UK. We were standing in the BIAP departure hall. You can imagine that even in its heyday, if it ever had one, it was not that opulent. They do have the world's cheapest Casio G Shock watches though, but that's another story.

I was looking out the window at the plane we would fly on. It was a commercial airliner operated by Jupiter Air and would get us to Dubai. It was dirty and ugly, with paint peeling off, and didn't seem to be in good repair. It didn't look too impressive and indeed was not. I didn't care though. It was the 'freedom bird'.

I heard a large, resonant boom sound come from somewhere outside. When you first hear a loud noise it is really hard to tell where it comes from. You usually have to wait until it is repeated to zero in on its source. In Australia, the first thing we would think, when we heard a loud noise, was that something large had fallen over at a building site, making a very loud noise. In Iraq you assume the worst. My eyes darted around the concrete apron, where a number of aircraft was parked. In the distance, about 500 metres away, I could see the telltale cloud of dust where a mortar round, or something similar, had landed. As I watched, another mortar round landed about 300 metres away. Oh no! I turned and headed away from the window towards the solid concrete portion of the building, which would offer some protection if the mortar crashed through the roof of the airport departure area. As I ran over, Todd, an Australian ex-soldier who was an old hand in Iraq, joined me. His presence, doing the same thing as me, convinced me that I had made the right choice. We crouched underneath the concrete roof and waited. I didn't feel safe, but I felt much safer. It's all relative.

The next mortar round boomed in, much closer. Debris flicked against the metal outside wall of the terminal building, as if somebody had thrown a handful of dirt at it. I hunched down lower and snuck a look over at the window. There was one of our team members, an ex-policeman from Victoria, standing at the window, craning his neck to get a better look at the explosions just outside.

I was stunned. Did he think the house-grade window glass would protect him from mortar rounds? Did he think that was just somebody letting off fireworks, ringing in the New Year a bit late perhaps? Did he realise he was still in Iraq? I was perplexed and concerned for his safety.

Boom! Another one came in. Really close. I was still pondering this guy's level of understanding when Todd yelled out, 'Fucking get away from that window!'

Actually, quite a few people, who had thought it was a good idea to look out the window, were startled by Todd's yelling. It was as if they had been in a stupor and Todd yelling out had broken the spell. Maybe they were like the fainting goats that go all stiff and fall over when you scare them. I don't know, but finally they scurried about, realising that they weren't just some onlookers, enjoying observer-only status, but were very likely to become extras in a horror film in the next few seconds. Perhaps it could be named Terminated at the Terminal or Terminal of Death, since Terminal Velocity is already taken.

The next round landed impotently on the concrete, making

the window shudder violently, but not break. That was it. Attack over. It was quiet for a few seconds and that was it. I knew that whoever had fired those rounds were probably within 5–7 kilometres of the airport, and they were now feverishly packing their gear and driving away. They knew, like all of us did, that the American direction-finding software was calculating a range and direction to them right now, and would soon send a response force out to remonstrate with them. The insurgency in Iraq is very adept at shooting at people from a distance, planting roadside bombs and encouraging suicide bombers to give their lives for the cause, but is totally incapable of mounting a stand-up fight with the American forces. I didn't blame them. If I was them, I would be running, fast.

In a few seconds a Russian stewardess (I realised she was Russian later) came out of our plane which was sitting on the tarmac, walked around it having a cursory look, and got back on. Twenty minutes later I boarded. Obviously, the plane had passed the stewardess's rigorous post-mortar-attack safety examination. Clearly she was a highly trained aeronautical engineer and structural damage expert. She certainly looked it as she walked around the plane in her short skirt and high heels. All good then, no need to worry.

Need to pay attention though.

It is not only war zones where you need to pay attention. Sometimes, you need to be on your game even in idyllic holiday resorts.

MANICURED

I travelled to Vanuatu to attend the beautiful marriage ceremony of some friends. The magnificent tropical setting, generous and happy local people, and terrific couple, surrounded by friends and family, really made it a memorable trip.

Trevor, one of our mates, had accompanied us. Now Trevor is a wildcard. Always has been, and I hope, always will be. He is not dangerous or malicious—ever—just hard to tie down and always up for trouble. I recall lying near the pool at a resort in Vanuatu, next to a perfectly manicured lawn and tropical flower garden, when my relaxation was disturbed by the unmistakable sound of a two-stroke engine. I looked up in time to see Trevor ride, sideways and almost out of control, down the hill, through the flowers, only to ultimately crash the motor scooter within inches of the pool. He got up, parked the scooter next to the pool and ordered a drink. If I had done that the two biggest security guards they could find would have ejected me, and I probably would have lost my wallet and one shoe in the process. Not so with Trevor. He was charming and likeable. I bet the security guards, had they come, would have wagged a finger at him, giggled, and walked away shaking their heads.

While we had been at home preparing for the trip, Trevor and I had been doing a fair bit of diving. I should say snorkelling, as we hadn't used scuba equipment but had enjoyed the sport of seeing how far, how long and how deep we could go on only one breath of air. It was an exhilarating and liberating endeavour, especially after having scuba-dived for a few years. We had a system where one diver would begin his descent and the other would remain on the surface to make sure he was alright. There is a condition called shallow water blackout, which afflicts divers. SWB causes the diver to suddenly lose consciousness in the last part of their ascent, and, if they are by themselves, they usually die. If a partner is watching it is a relatively easy rescue. If you can bring them to the surface, they will live. So it is good practice to operate this way, and it could be a lifesaver.

We had generally been doing our diving in the cold waters of Port Phillip Bay, in Victoria, with occasional forays outside the bay on the east coast of Victoria. Our practice was paying off and our endurance and ability was better every time we hit the water.

In Vanuatu we were keen to hit the water. The whole crew went out on a charter boat to better see the islands. It was a good-sized cruiser and Trevor and I had talked to the crew about taking us out in the boat's tender and finding a good place for a dive.

It was an awesome day on the water, windless, no swell, clear skies and a powerful overhead sun. Two crewmen took Trevor and me to a wonderful spot, over a colourful reef with occasional sandy patches and teeming with fish. When we stopped I put on my mask and leant over the side. I pulled my head out and told Trevor what I had seen. We both broke the record for getting our gear on in a hurry, and slipped over the side.

It was traditional for us to go straight to the bottom and return with a handful of sand to prove you had 'sounded', meaning you got to the bottom. I looked at the bottom and thought it was about 12 to 15 metres deep. No worries. I had guessed the depth by judging how clearly I could make out objects and fish swimming near the bottom. In this case,

I could make out those objects really easily. I took a few deep breaths and duck-dived down towards the bottom, aiming at a nice sandy patch where a few fish lazily swam in circles. I started long easy strokes on my fins, to conserve energy and take it easy, as this was my first dive, but 12 to 15 metres was easily within my range. After a few seconds I felt like I was hardly making any progress towards the bottom. I attributed this to the fact that I was using a different weight belt than I usually would, and had just roughly estimated how much weight I would require, seeing as I was not wearing a wetsuit as you do every day in Victoria. I raised my kick rate right up and got into a nice efficient form.

After a few more seconds I thought, really, I'm not going as quickly as I should be, I'm getting closer, but not quickly enough. This time I attributed it to the fact that I was wearing borrowed fins, and they weren't as efficient and stiff as the fins I usually use. I pushed on.

A few more seconds after that I was at the bottom. I was starting to get that feeling of wanting a breath of air, so was glad to be there. Ah, success! I triumphantly scooped up a handful of sand and flipped my body to push off the sea floor with my legs. I looked up and was immediately terrified by the vista that awaited me. I was way deeper than I had ever been on a breath of air, and, remember, still only at the half-way point. As I looked above at the reflective underside of the ocean I felt like I had never seen so much ocean surface in my life. I was really terrified and knew I needed to stay calm, but work hard for the surface and that next, beautiful breath of air. The ocean surface seemed to stretch out above me in all directions for hundreds of metres. The water was like crystal, and I suddenly understood my mistake. From the surface, I was able to make out objects on the sea floor in fine detail because of the crystalline water and strong penetration of the overhead light. All of my practice for this trip had been in the decidedly brackish and cold waters of Victoria, where the sun doesn't penetrate very deeply and underwater visibility of 10 metres is exceptional. I had been descending at the normal rate, but had gone a lot further than normal. I estimated that I was down about 25 to 30 metres. Too far.

I focused on Trevor, bobbing on the surface above me, and pushed off hard, getting every advantage I could from the ocean floor, which I, unfairly, felt nothing but contempt for. Soon I was halfway up and really feeling the need to get a new dose of that life-giving air in my lungs. I didn't know whether Trevor had recognised the danger, but, as I ascended, I meekly gave him the thumbs-up in case he had caught on to the situation and had become worried.

At about 5 metres I knew I was safe, if I didn't black out. I burst through the surface and inhaled a lung full of beautiful air as I momentarily rose out of the water. I reached across to Trevor, but he was gone, dropping into his descent. I tried to chase him and grab hold of his fin to turn him around and explain, but in my currently weakened form I had no hope. I watched anxiously as Trevor slowly descended, and thought that he was probably having exactly the same thoughts that I did, and that in a moment he would be confronted by the same scene that I was.

And so it was. I watched as Trevor turned on the bottom,

and jolted with the sudden realisation of his advanced and possibly dire depth. He rocketed off the bottom in the same manner that I did, and soon held out the telltale thumbs-up to let me know he was still OK. I was pretty much fully recovered and thinking about the possible need to rescue Trevor, in the case of a SWB. He was now in the last but most dangerous section. He broke the surface, grabbed his breath and let fly.

'Why didn't you tell me it was so deep?'

'What? Do you reckon that was deep, Trev?'

Should have paid attention. We took it easy from then on.

This stuff is important. I have seen too many mistakes or near disasters because of not paying attention to our surroundings. I try to do things differently now. I plan, I sit back and observe, and I pay attention.

Still, I will get caught out again sometime.

Not on fire

ON FIRE!

CHAPTER 9

Battle inoculation

'If you can keep your head, while all those around you are losing theirs and blaming it on you, then you probably don't understand the situation.'

I like that quote, and I'm pretty sure I heard it from Paul Hogan, but he might not have been the first person to pervert the words from Kipling's famous poem, *If*. It's a good point though, and there are only two ways to stay calm in a crisis. The first is to be so ignorant that you don't know that you are in a crisis, and the second way is absolutely and unshakably knowing you can get yourself out of the crisis. If you are in the second category, you are way ahead.

The ability to remain calm comes from a number of different sources. The most common source is generally being self-confident. This is a good one, because it can be transposed onto most situations. When you are physically fit and mentally agile, you become a lot closer to being unflappable than most people. Another good source of calm, at least outwardly, is being vain enough to want to appear calm. Believe me, when you appear calm, you gradually become calm, even if you were faking it. One of the Indian chiefs, I think it was Chief Sitting

Bull, used to say to his warriors before battle, 'I don't require you to be brave, just act brave.' He was chief for a very good reason, not just because he had the most feathers.

The other way we get through personal disasters calmly is by following processes. That is, having a predetermined action we will take in the case of × happening, and then sticking to that plan with the faith that it will work. I have seen that work very effectively time and time again. Having a plan is never bad.

However, far and away the most important factor in dealing with an emergency calmly is having experience or exposure to calamities and critical situations. If you have been through it, you know you will survive and are much more confident in your abilities. Exposure to emergencies, in general, helps you in any new type of calamity, so the knowledge, if that's what you would like to call it, is transferable between events. In the military they call this exposure 'Battle Inoculation', and I reckon it is a highly appropriate and clever term.

So, yeah, sorry, but in my experience there is nothing like, errr, experience.

Keeping calm is important. There are lots of ways to describe your best reaction to an emergency, but we can encapsulate them all by saying 'Keep calm'. Keeping calm allows you to take in all the available information. When we panic or get highly excited (the same thing, on a physiological level), then our bodies start to do things that hinder our ability to get the information we should.

We get what is referred to as auditory exclusion, where we effectively shut off input from our ears. Our body believes that in an emergency you really only need to rely on visual input, so shuts down the circuit to your ears. In some highly stressful situations you will ask somebody a question, and they will seemingly ignore you, but really it is just their circuitry re-filing your request under 'maybe later'.

Ok, well, that might seem fine, but our eyes, or at least the analysis of the input from our eyes, doesn't work to full capacity when we are overly excited either. Our eyes decide to prioritise the scene directly in front, giving us a form of unconscious and self-imposed tunnel vision. It is thought that this allows us to judge distance more accurately, but I won't be chalking that up as an advantage in most cases. This is annoying too, because we need to retain our broader and indeed peripheral vision in an emergency.

I should make it clear, if it isn't already, that these are not physical changes in the way our eyes or ears work, but in the ways in which the data that they collect is analysed by our brains.

There are other physiological changes too. Our heart and breathing rates go up. We feel the energising effect of adrenaline pulsing through us. This, of course, is our body preparing for fight or flight.

These physiological changes also make it more difficult for us to analyse the imperfect, or at least incomplete, information that we have been provided by our now recalcitrant eyes and ears.

We are on the back foot from the start then.

Obviously, when we are confronted by an emergency, that is exactly when we need all the information we can get, and need to make good, grounded decisions.

ARMOURED VEHICLES

In the next situation, I bet I went through the full range of physiological reactions to stress, and probably a few new ones too.

It was pretty much at the height of the sectarian violence in Iraq, in 2007. On this occasion I was employed as a private security contractor, and my team would travel about 250 kilometres from our base south of Baghdad, to Baghdad, and then to the Baghdad International Air Port. Our job, on these occasions, was to ferry our staff from the work site to Baghdad and then BIAP. There was usually a team of about eleven or twelve guys, all quite experienced policemen or soldiers or both.

Iraq was a very dangerous place, at least where we were driving around. We would use three armoured vehicles. Two were large Revas. These are big, black, South African-designed, menacing monsters built on a truck chassis. They were hard to drive, slow, noisy and uncomfortable but—and this is a huge but—well armoured and well armed. We would man two machine guns in turrets in each Reva. This gave us an enormous amount of firepower. You would need to be pretty desperate for targets to decide to take us on while we drove around in these things. The third vehicle was a bit different. It was a Toyota Landcruiser, which was just as armoured as the Revas but could only aim a gun from its rear, where the normal tailgate had been removed and replaced with a plate of armour, with a slot for shooting out of.

I was posted on the front machine gun in the turret of one of the Revas. My job was to look out for any vehicles approaching from the front that posed a threat of attack. We prided ourselves on a certain reservation about shooting at anyone. I say at, because we avoided shooting at anyone as much as we could, and the vast amount of shots fired were warning shots to get the errant person or vehicle to rethink their actions before we all had to do something we would regret. I personally think this reserved style was the best way to operate, and while it may not have been in favour with the various cowboys getting around Iraq, it fitted very well, morally, with our predominantly Australian team.

I was covered head to toe in Nomex, which is a fire-retardant material similar in feel and appearance to cotton. I had a Nomex flight suit, balaclava and gloves to protect me from flames and flash burning. I had ballistic goggles on and a Kevlar helmet and bulletproof vest. My outfit would never get me a cover shot for a men's fashion magazine, but it was the very height of fashion for those in my line of work. I was manning a Belgian-made Mag 58 machine gun. It was a large heavy gun, accurate and reliable, and we carried in excess of 10 000 rounds of ammunition for the two guns. As well as the Mag 58 I had my personal weapon, a Colt M4 5.56-mm calibre assault rifle attached to me by a sling. I carried ten 30-round magazines for the M4 on my ballistic vest. Then, last, and very much least, I carried a Glock 19 9-mm pistol and three 15-round magazines for it. I had two fragmentation grenades and two smoke grenades in an easy-to-reach spot on the vest. I also carried a radio, torch, knife, water, and a distress beacon on my vest. The vest itself had Kevlar weave material inside and two heavy steel plates, front and rear. I suppose the vest probably weighed around 12 to 15 kilos. The rifle weighed about 2–3 kilos and the machine gun about 11 kilos. Overall it was heavy enough that I was glad that I rarely had to lug it all around.

My relationship with my ballistic vest is a strange thing. (Don't go off on a wrong tangent here.) In Australia we have a plant that grows wild in grazing areas. It's called Paterson's Curse. But, rather intriguingly, it can also be known as Salvation Jane. The curse bit comes from the fact that it's a particularly hardy plant and grows right over normal field grasses, ultimately starving them. It isn't a great form of feed for grazing animals. Therefore in a good season, it is always called Paterson's Curse for the effect it has on farmers' crops. The salvation bit is different. In a bad season, something else happens. I said it was particularly hardy, so even when the normal grass crops have failed there is still Paterson's Curse to be found. Of course, in these seasons it is known by the much more respectful name of Salvation Jane. Though it is a meagre source of food compared to grass when there is no grass, Salvation Jane may just save the day for a hungry herd.

The same goes for my ballistic vest. On good days it was heavy, uncomfortable and hot. You peeled it off and threw it down in a heap as soon as possible after work. On bad days though, when it was a bulletproof barrier and covered in the accoutrements of battle/survival, it was suddenly as light as a feather, indispensable and as comforting as a child's security blanket. Strange that.

On the rear machine gun on my Reva was Dodge, a great bloke with a sharp sense of humour and easy, relaxed style. We exchanged glances as we swept through the arcs of travel of our turrets, usually nodding, as you couldn't see facial expressions through the Nomex hoods. We both had headphones on that cancelled out really loud outside noises, in case there was an explosion or gunfire, and our radios were in an earpiece inside the headphones. This was a great system, as even when driving along with the heavy wind noise, we could clearly hear normal conversation on the radio.

On this particular day we had a great run to Baghdad. By that, I mean no roadside bombs, no hold-ups with convoys or unexpected detours. There had been some loud cracks while we were still out on a broad highway, which indicated that somebody may have fired at us from a distance, but it was not too disconcerting. It just prompted Dodge and I to have a good critical sweep through all the possible firing positions close by. Nothing seen and no need to fire off any rounds, so we did not divert or carry out any defensive manoeuvres at all. We had no passengers onboard, as we were only transiting to Baghdad to work there for a few days, ferrying people to the airport and back, before returning to the base in south central Iraq.

It was hot, around 40–45 degrees Celsius, and we were highly alert as we entered the battle-scarred suburbs of Baghdad. On the outskirts of Baghdad we travelled through a particularly dangerous area called Iskandariah. This was a centre for Iraqi militant fighters, and attacks on convoys like ours, and coalition military assets, were daily events. We drove quickly through Iskandariah, but, having made it through without incident, did not dare to relax. I always found it easy to stay alert in Baghdad, as it was not a place that let you rest for a second, even though armoured and well armed; it purveyed a simmering tension at all times. I have described being in the Red Zone in Baghdad as like standing near an electricity transformer as it buzzes. You feel the electricity in your skin, the buzz deep in your body, and there is a huge menacing power just barely contained in the wires that threatens you, without words or gestures. Sounds nice, doesn't it?

Baghdad looked like it had been constructed from porous mud bricks and sand-coloured concrete. There was little stylistic or colouration difference between one house and the next, or indeed shops or industrial buildings for that matter. The streets were covered in litter and dust. Dust was everywhere and ground its way insidiously into everything around you. Even if the buildings and streets had been in perfect order, they would have been drab and quickly uninteresting. As it was, they were in terrible disrepair. Some were battle damaged and even if the damage to buildings was not directly the result of fighting, it was certainly caused by the war zone environment. Repairs were rarely carried out, and building materials were hard to come by and expensive. No civil authority cleaned the streets and the people had to live their lives in terribly difficult conditions without all the amenities we take for granted in the 'Global North'. Most of Baghdad had no power or water, or only intermittent services of one or both.

Adding insult to injury, a convoy of foreigners drove through the neighbourhood in large armoured vehicles, blithely pointing weapons at anyone who looked at them. Unfortunately the 'them' in this case was us.

We were going really well. We weren't far from Checkpoint 12 which was the entrance to the fabled coalition military-controlled Green Zone, which affords secure protection to the many foreign residents of Baghdad. We were driving down off an overpass when a strong vibration could be felt right through the vehicle. It felt like one of the wheels was no longer round, and quickly got worse until it made the whole vehicle shudder. I heard the driver of the vehicle behind us call on the radio and say there was smoke coming out from beneath our vehicle. I turned around and looked past Dodge and could see an impressive plume of thick black smoke trailing us. Our driver, Schippy, was onto it. He called through the radio, his voice calm, 'This is Zulu 2, I see the smoke. We will try to make it to the Green Zone and then put it out.'

Fair enough, I thought. This was still a bad neighbourhood and I didn't fancy stopping here at all.

An armoured vehicle in this situation is like a wounded animal, likely to attract all manner of predators. So we pushed on.

A few seconds later and the vibration turned into a clanging of metal against metal. It felt like a violent mechanical catastrophe in the undercarriage of the vehicle.

Over the radio I heard a voice from the Landcruiser behind us. 'This is Zulu 3. Zulu 2, you need to stop and put that fire out immediately.'

Then Schippy's voice once more through the radio. Still calm and in control. 'This is Zulu 2, we have lost all brakes on this vehicle.'

There was no panic, it was as if he was relaying information about his latest haircut, not the fate of the entire crew on the vehicle. Even though we were still doing about 80–90 kilometres per hour, I thought, yeah, no problems, he'll just downshift through the gears to stop us. Easy.

A few more seconds and, 'This is Zulu 2, our steering and transmission have gone.'

Um, yeah, that is more of a problem. We were on a stretch of road that was like a freeway, with Armco Barriers on both sides.

Then immediately after Schippy's latest bad news: 'This is Zulu 3. Guys, you really need to stop that vehicle immediately and put the fire out.'

There was still no panic in anybody's voice.

Schippy wrestled the vehicle, without the assistance of the power steering, and deliberately crashed into the Armco Barrier in an attempt to slow us down. We graunched along the barrier and it appeared to be working. It was a huge heavy vehicle and was taking a lot of slowing down, but Schippy was a great driver and I had every confidence in his skills and experience driving the Reva.

I looked ahead to a large gap in the Armco where it had been destroyed by an earlier collision of some type. We had slowed down but now scraped our way into the gap, approaching the point where the damaged Armco started again.

Over the radio: 'Brace. Brace. Brace.'

We crashed heavily into the Armco and ground to a halt. Dodge and I were thrown about a bit in the turrets, but were OK. I had a look around and said to Dodge, 'Mate, I reckon we should stay up here while they put the fire out, as security.'

I knew that the guys trying to fight the fire would have their attention on putting out that fire and not on securing our position on the road. We swung our guns around in threatening arcs, dissuading anyone from having too close a look at what was going on.

Every time the guys fighting the fire stopped spraying it with the chemical fire extinguishers, it instantly engulfed the underside of the vehicle again.

I heard over the radio, 'Get everyone off that vehicle.'

There was only Dodge and I left, as Matt, the vehicle commander, and Schippy had got out straight after it stopped to fight the fire. I looked around and was reluctant to get off. I thought that the fire would be out in a second, and didn't want to give up my commanding view of the area and therefore excellent firing position. Looking down I could see a lot of fire coming up from the righthand side of the vehicle. I gave it a few more seconds then yelled over to Dodge, 'Time to go I reckon.'

I stripped about 150 rounds off the bandolier that was attached to my Mag 58 and took out the retaining pins. There was no way I was leaving it to be burnt, or fall into the hands of terrorists. I went to get out of the turret and down and out through the inside of the vehicle, but had clearly left my run too late. The passenger compartment was extensively on fire and filled with smoke. The other option was to climb out over the top and down the left side, which did not seem so engulfed by flames. It suddenly occurred to me that my flameproof suit had actually come in very handy for once. (I guess it only has to save you once.)

I jumped up on the top of the vehicle but could not jump onto the bonnet, as I usually would, as the engine compartment was now fully ablaze. That meant I had to climb down the side to about halfway, and jump from there. I hit the ground next to the left side luggage compartment. I opened it up and grabbed my pack. I slung it over one shoulder and ran forward to take up a firefighting position in the gutter about 20 metres to the front of the now totally engulfed Reva. Looking back I could see that even now the left side of the vehicle was totally engulfed. I had got off (and saved my pack) just in time.

In a few more seconds it was obvious that the fire had won. I was somewhat startled to hear ammunition already cooking off and exploding inside the vehicle, only a minute or two after I had contemplated going out through the rear door. My legs had been dangling inside that compartment moments ago. It was time to leave, the vehicle would not be salvaged and we were very vulnerable to attack. The other Reva, Zulu 1, reversed back from the security position it had taken up, and we piled into the back. Within a few seconds we were all onboard and the now reduced convoy continued on to Checkpoint 12 and the relative safety of the Green Zone.

No injuries, no opportunistic attack by the militants. Despite the enormous number of things that could have gone horribly wrong, the team worked together, stayed calm and resolute, and got everyone out safely.

When we examined the incident later, and looked at all the contributing facts and circumstances, we concluded that two factors contributed to team success. The first was the level of experience of individual team members. All had been in Iraq for a minimum of ten months, some up to three years. All had military or police experience, making them familiar with complex divided-attention tasking during emergencies.

The other important factor was reliance on processes. We had practised many times moving a crew to another vehicle, during circumstances of compromised security, because of breakdown or battle damage. Knowledge of the drill made us confident that the supporting team members would act in a certain way, and therefore gave a sense of calm to our actions, despite the dangerous location and circumstances.

The other thing that struck me about this incident was that twenty minutes after we had barely escaped with our lives, in a war zone, we were all sipping lattes in the relative comfort and safety of the Green Zone. What a weird place.

Recognising the physiological effects of stress on yourself can be difficult. Recognising it in somebody else is usually easy.

In Timor-Leste in 2006 I was the program manager for Australian Aid International's response to the rioting and civil conflict in that country. We flew in and very quickly established a medical service for local people caught up in the violence. We worked in conjunction with a large Australian NGO that had long-established development programs in Timor but no emergency response capability.

This was, and is, a new country, only having gained independence from Indonesia in 2002, and still finding its way as a player in the Pacific and South-East Asia. Timor-Leste, formerly known as East Timor, has had a difficult time in the last few years. In 2006 the leaders of the small, resource-rich country were undergoing a power struggle, and, like always, the poor and unempowered ultimately bore the brunt of the effects. The country was in a confusing turmoil, centred in the capital, Dili. The streets of Dili were overrun with rioters, going on an arson binge every afternoon and evening. There were a number of deaths and serious injuries associated with the violence but I eventually had the feeling that the vast majority of rioters, on both sides of the argument, wanted to get their message across and convey their menace, but did not want to kill people to express their frustration.

Our medical team had a great Toyota Landcruiser, on loan from the Australian military, and travelled around to assist groups of people who were refugees from the violence. Refugees set up camps in any place they felt safe: outside the Australian Embassy, a park in the middle of town, and church grounds. About 70 000 people were displaced and a huge humanitarian disaster loomed.

A number of times we were positioned close to the rioting and a few times became embroiled in the quickly changing crowds. On all those occasions I felt safe. Throngs of protestors and rioters would come past, and, if they acknowledged us at all, were joyful and often shouted 'Viva Australia!' when they saw the Australian flag on our vehicle. The Portuguese press, at the time, was making out that a great deal of the frustration was because of Australian colonialist intentions, but that just wasn't evident anywhere I went. I think it was more of an attractive tagline for a Portuguese newspaper than a reality in the former Portuguese colony that was now looking like a failed state.

Well, we had been in Timor for about two weeks and the

rioting ebbed and flowed, with no clear winner but many losers. As well as the strictly medical staff, I was there with another friend of mine, Gav, who had solid military experience and all-round life experience. My friend Paul, of the Pakistan trip, also accompanied us to report to the UN and attend meetings etc. We had made sure that the headquarters of the NGO that had requested our presence was secure, and staff were briefed on what to do if the rioting threatened their safety. It is not being chauvinistic to say that we presented as a male-dominated team of ex-soldiers/police who were generally medically trained, so the female-dominated development-based NGO that we worked with was very happy that we were there to support them. I am not for a moment implying that they were incapable or shrinking violets in any way. These ladies were highly independent and seasoned internationalists, but rioting and killing nearby shakes anyone's confidence. We tried to put back some of that confidence. Their own security officer was a young guy, overwhelmed by the circumstances, untrained and largely out of his depth. The national level of disorder and obvious breakdown of the rule of law was not his cup of tea. Tough luck, he still had a responsible job to perform. Welcome to A-Grade competition, son. We found ourselves developing procedures for staff to follow during any emergency and generally tried to give people the confidence to continue their important work with the community.

Our liaison with that Australian NGO was a dedicated and enthusiastic lady from Australia called Kat. She had been staying at a secure hotel, where our team was located, but had decided that the situation was calm enough for her to move back to her house in one of Dili's suburbs, where she lived with two other young women, one European, one American. I admired her spirit, but ultimately didn't think it was that good an idea.

One night soon after she moved back, Gav, Paul and I were having dinner in a bar in Dili, as the food shops were not yet open, so choices were limited. It was about 8.30 PM and a sort of undeclared curfew stopped most people from moving about. My phone rang and it was Kat, in a high state of panic. I couldn't really understand what she was saying, but she was terrified, and the level of fright she imparted with her tone really gave me pause. I reached out and tapped Gav on the shoulder, and pointed to the phone. I wanted his attention, and Paul stopped talking too.

This was one of those times when a calm voice on the other end of the line was going to make a big difference to her demeanour, and allow me to get an idea of what was going on. I had been in this situation many times, taking calls from panicked members of the public as a police officer, and turned it on, speaking slowly and deliberately and with a sense of familiarity, as if everything was OK.

'Kat, just slow down a bit, mate, I couldn't quite hear what you said.'

Her voice was better, but still not good, but what she did say gave me reason to worry.

'They're attacking the house. I can hear gunshots and bombs, Nathan. They've started a fire outside.'

'OK, Kat. Have you rung the army?'

The Australian Army had a Quick Reaction Force that was

on standby for situations like this. They were well armed, disciplined and aggressive, and the rioters knew not to mess with them. I had quite a few mates serving with that unit in Timor. Since then, from talking to locals, I have found out that they had an enviable reputation. They were differentiated from the normal soldiers by carrying M4 rifles that were plain black, as opposed to the normal issue Steyr rifle that was green and black. Because of this, they were known as the Black Guns, and usually news of their arrival at a scene broke up a crowd.

'Nathan, they're too busy. Nobody is coming to help,' Kat said, her voice again sounding panicked.

I could hear loud bangs in the background and men shouting. None of the bangs really sounded like gunfire to me, but I was hearing them down a mobile phone connection. Actually, it sounded serious, and I was somewhat worried for her safety. I knew the army was flat out and had another ten incidents, probably just like this one, to deal with.

Kat was frantic. 'What should we do?'

I wasn't sure. But I knew I had to seem confident. I had to let her question hang for a moment while I had a think.

Really, I thought it highly unlikely that the crowd around her house had armed themselves with guns or bombs and had suddenly decided, in a bloodthirsty rage, that they needed to kill three young humanitarians. It would have been totally out of kilter with the rest of the rioting and demonstrations. It just didn't seem likely, regardless of how real it sounded down the phone line. I thought, we have to try to get there; even if we can't get all the way to the house, we might be able to see what's going on and make some calls and get this incident bumped up on the army's priority list.

'Hold tight and we'll come and get you. I'll ring you in a couple of minutes for an update. Pack some things and get everyone else ready. You should all leave together. Turn your lights out and stay away from the windows until we're there. We're five minutes away.'

That was what she needed: relief, somebody with a plan, a job to busy herself with, and light at the end of a dark tunnel. She was much happier and calmer immediately. 'OK, thanks, Nathan.'

I turned to Gav and Paul.

'We have to get Kat and her housemates and it doesn't sound too good. She mentioned shooting and explosions. I could hear loud bangs but it didn't sound like gunshots to me. What do you reckon?'

I looked at the guys, plaintively I suppose, waiting to get their reaction. They had heard me tell Kat that we would come and get her, but I wasn't going to drag anyone into something like this unwillingly. Gav immediately stood up, and Paul said 'Let's go' without a moment's hesitation.

Paul really impressed me with his go-hard attitude. Actually, he always had. He was not one of the army-type guys, didn't beat his chest or make an over-the-top impression, but he didn't hesitate that night, when asked to put himself on the line. Later I thought about the events and realised that by going with Gav and me, Paul had stepped WAY outside his comfort zone. He had no military or emergency services training and had been exposed to very few critical incidents, but there he was, all 'Let's get her!', and, yeah, that impressed me.

DEAD ENDS

Gav drove. He nearly always did. He was a terrific driver and knew his way around four-wheel drives very well. He had also really quickly got the knack of driving the confusing streets of Dili. Some streets are one-way, then abruptly revert to being two-way; some streets are virtual dead ends; and every street looks very similar – shambolic with burnt-out houses and shops everywhere.

I said earlier that the Toyota Landcruiser Troop Carrier we had on loan from the Australian Army was great and there was a good reason for that. Not only are they a large, robust, powerful, spartan vehicle, but ours looked exactly like what the Black Guns of the Australian Special Forces drove around in. At night this was invaluable, and sometimes we traded on our resemblance to the Australian Army Quick Reaction Force. This was to be one of those nights. All we really had to do was drive fast and use the high beams so nobody could really see who was driving. Perfect.

The suburbs of Dili had been divided up, roughly, into various factions. Poorly constructed roadblocks were down many streets. Really, we weren't the intended targets of these impromptu roadblocks and we were never detained or even questioned at the odd checkpoint that was manned. They could see we were not looters or rioters and assumed, rightly, that we had only good intentions, so always let us straight through. The roadblocks were usually only a couple of drums and a piece of wood, or a few large pieces of concrete spread over the road.

We drove towards the few roadblocks on the way to Kat's house at great speed and convinced anyone around who stepped onto the road that to challenge us was a bad idea. I would say that a Landcruiser Troop Carrier has rarely travelled across Dili at such a speed. Black Hawk helicopters flew overhead, in support of troop actions on the ground. My only worry was that we might drive right into some battle between factions or against some of the security forces.

I called Kat and she told me that there was still a lot of shouting outside and the occasional loud bang. There was a large fire on the road and lots of people milling around. She had the lights off and the girls were waiting at the door near the driveway, with the door locked until I personally spoke through the door to them. Nobody was injured, and everything looked OK.

Kat's street had a slight uphill and a number of turns and we roared up and stopped suddenly after each turn to illuminate the street ahead before committing to it any further. It was a great move as it allowed us to look down the street and have a quick listen out for anything we should know about.

Everything seemed pretty good so Gav roared through the last bend in a low gear, to keep the engine revving nice and high and hopefully scare Christ out of anyone still around. It worked. As we came around the corner we could see the last few guys disappear into the ether off the side of the road. There was a fire burning in the middle of the road outside Kat's place, but the firelighters had abandoned the scene.

We pulled up in front of the house. Gav deftly swung the Troopy around and reversed up the driveway. I got out at the bottom of the driveway and had a good look around before I declared the area safe for the girls to unlatch the door.

I walked up to the doorway and called out for Kat. Paul had the rear doors of the Troopy open and the three girls filed out, in a low crouch, and jumped in the back. They were travelling light and had limited themselves to small bags and a few possessions. I had a last look around the area and shut the back door. We still had to get back to the Venture Hotel, a well-secured place with nice high walls.

The drive back mirrored the drive to Kat's house and was largely uneventful. Kat and her friends were pretty shell-shocked by what had occurred. They had felt like they were welcome in their local community and were very taken aback by the night's events. Fair enough.

We achieved what we had set out to do only through maintaining a degree of calmness. In this case the calm came from quickly and objectively reviewing the facts as reported to us from Kat (who had never faced a crisis like this, or likely any other) and comparing these to our experiences (having faced plenty of crises and having a feel for the current troubles). In the end, our instinct was right: nobody really wanted to attack and kill three young humanitarians who had done nothing but care for the local community. An act like that would have been abhorrent to anyone I knew then, or know now, in Timor.

In the morning we travelled back to the house with Kat to remove any other valuables and retrieve her car. Looking around the house, there were no bullet holes or damage from explosives.

I got in Kat's Nissan Micra and began driving it back to the hotel. Kat was in the passenger seat and I followed Gav, who was driving the Landcruiser. Kat was still shaken and fairly noncommunicative. I let her be. She looked like she was ready to cry. In a few minutes she spoke. 'Our neighbours wouldn't help us. I rang them. The army didn't help. You really never know who you can trust.'

It was just too corny for me to resist. So I said it. 'You do now.'

I bet I winked at her after that, then affected a steely look and went silent. It felt like something John Wayne would say in an old western movie. I'm surprised that I kept myself from bursting out laughing. Classic.

Stay calm, and everything will be alright. Well, stay calm anyway.

CHAPTER 10

Cultural differences

'Ahh, sorry, we don't do that here.'

I have travelled a fair bit, a lot really. I have been very lucky. However, I have never seen the Great Wall of China or the Eiffel Tower. Statue of Liberty—nope. Tower of London—no. Petronas Towers, ahh, no. Taj Mahal, guess not. Mecca, sorry, no. The Vatican, hmmm, never. Kruger National Park, nope, not yet. The Pyramids, nah. South/North Pole, not likely. Red Square, not me.

I was at a party a while ago, and somebody, who had heard I had been around, asked me about London, New York, Amsterdam, Tokyo, LA, Paris, Rome, Moscow, etc. Umm, sorry, never been there.

'Oh, I thought you were well-travelled.'

'I suppose not.'

I didn't bother explaining. I must admit, though, to feeling a bit smug, but I suppose he did too, so it was even.

Except—he was wrong.

I have been to a heap of places, in crises, wars, civil unrest, natural disasters and political upheaval. I have snuck into, or out of, at least three different countries and camped on the edge of mountains during earthquakes, under pieces of plastic during tropical storms, hidden in corners during rioting and stuck newspaper down my shirt for warmth, met rebel commanders and crime figures, masters of industry, hundreds and thousands of the poor, been shot at, blown up and otherwise attacked, and all the while felt good about it.

I don't travel to see things. Things don't really interest me that much. Though, I don't discount the beauty of so many amazing places in our world. I haven't seen them, but I'm quite certain that the Sistine Chapel is breathtaking and the Grand Canyon awe-inspiring. I will see them later, after I'm past running with the disasters.

When I go somewhere new, it's not the objects or natural wonders in that place that intrigue me, it's the people. I suppose what really takes my interest is that I compare them to me. I see the multitude of ways we are the same, and the important ways we are different. I don't mean physically different, for the physical differences are slight, and we tend to be fairly expert in identifying them by the time we're fifteen, if you grow up in Australia, or anywhere in the Western world. I couldn't tell you how many anthropological documentaries I watched when I was a kid. I think, in lieu of international travel, my parents made me watch them so I would understand a bit about the world, and my very fortunate, and small, place in it. It was a great idea. When I travel, I see the people. I see the different thought processes that different people around the world have. I reckon this will keep me interested for the rest of my life.

If I accept, and I do, that we are pretty much all the same model human, with a few minor detail changes and outside colour variations, then I reckon we all have the same brain.

So, if we all have the same computer up there, it must be the software we have loaded onto it that makes us different. How do we load that software? Well, I reckon it's a long process that undergoes many auto-updates, and we call it culture. We absorb it as a free download from our surroundings, and it is always appropriate to our individual environment.

The bulk of my travel has really been done in response to humanitarian disasters. This has put me in situations where I have seen desperate humans struggling to survive. It is in these situations that I have experienced the greatest acts of charity and examples of humanity. We truly are incredible beasts, and we should work to value the lives of humankind extremely highly. We need to recognise the differences in people, and then go on to figure out why we are different, and, ultimately, value those differences.

When you go abroad, remember, they are not different to you, you are different to them.

While I was with the Australian Army in Bougainville, Papua New Guinea, we had an enforced period of leave. Everyone I knew took his or her four days of leave at the Australian Base HQ at a place called Loloho. It was comfortable there, with movies and a little shop, and lots of other people to talk to. I think the main attraction for people was airconditioning and other Aussies to talk to. I didn't begrudge people their decision to go there, but thought a great deal about my options.

I didn't want to go to Loloho. I wanted to go and stay in a

remote village somewhere. Nobody else had ever suggested such a thing. It just wasn't the usual thing for soldiers to wish to take their leave in a remote village, somewhere they had to be during work periods, when they could have spent their leave luxuriating in airconditioning, watching movies and eating ice-cream.

My friend Tim (from the Great Rubbish Pit Explosion Incident) and I hatched a plan. We would write a letter to a chief on one of the offshore islands near Bougainville, asking if we could stay at his village for our leave. We would bring him some sort of tribute and food and all he had to do was let us stay within the confines of the village. The Australian Air Force helicopter crew who did the rounds of the communities, dropping information about the peace process, delivered the letter. Eventually we got a letter back from the gracious Chief Laiben Goresua, of Rautan Island, allowing us to visit the island. The island is about 1 kilometre off the southeast coast of Bougainville. It was a great letter, using formal language befitting a chief, but in simple English with a bit of Tok Pisin thrown in. One of the last lines in the letter said, 'Everything is just OK tasol.'

That does not sound too good in English, but in Tok Pisin that means everything is perfect. The word tasol literally means that's all (say it fast) and means nothing else has to be said. To say everything is just OK means that, really, everything is great. Happily we had our permission and made ready for our trip.

We dragged another bloke along with us and it was epic. We choppered in and landed on a beach, as there was nowhere else to get the chopper down. The village community looked after us like long-lost sons and we felt right at home. They built us a hut on the beach and cooked fish and lobster for us all day. Tim and I spent our days snorkelling around the incredible reef on which the island had been formed. Tim had a long spear gun and shaft from home and it was a ripper.

The people on Rautan Island were happy, and, we discovered, largely insulated from the crisis and civil war that had enveloped the main island. That 1-kilometre stretch of water from the main island was just far enough to allow them to stay uninvolved in the violence. They didn't know too much about the way people like us lived our lives, but they lived pretty good lives themselves. They made a great living by catching and farming crocodiles and sharks and collecting sea cucumbers and large sea snails for trade with Korean and Indonesian fishermen.

The men dived all day. They had homemade spear guns, and usually they just wore these bad goggles that were crappy the day they were made, and now, ten years later, were next to useless. They must have made fishing for your livelihood very difficult. The whole village of more than 100 people had two sets of diving fins and these were in equally poor shape. Tim and I hatched a plan to give the chief's son, Ben, our diving equipment when we left. Ben and his wife, Eunice, had looked after us terrifically, and Ben had been our liaison, of sorts, a guide and protector who made sure we had everything we needed. He was a great guy. He was massive, heavily muscled and super fit from diving in the ocean all day and doing manual labour around the village. We knew Ben would give the equipment out in a fair and reasonable way to other people in the village. My fins were Australian Army issue, so cost me nothing, and my mask was a personal one from home, but easy to replace.

On the second last day I approached Ben and handed over my fins. He was highly embarrassed, and would not take them. On his island, diving fins like these were very valuable because they would increase the success of the user in catching fish. So it was really hard for him to accept such a valuable gift. They were obviously also really hard to come by on his island, with no shops or any way of purchasing goods like that. He really believed that I would be lost without these fins, and would not accept them as a gift. After about twenty minutes of negotiation he finally accepted. I went back and told Tim, and we decided that we would need a better plan for giving the rest of our gear away. We thought the best way was to just leave it behind and not get into an argument at all.

The next morning the chopper came to pick us up and we loaded our packs onboard. No worries. We had left behind our diving equipment: another pair of fins, two masks, a dive knife and, best of all, the very nice spear shaft from Tim's spear gun. Well, we got on the chopper, did our belts up and were ready to take off. Then the chief's son came running up to the helicopter, and bundled in his arms was the diving gear. He obviously thought that we had forgotten it. He was trying to load it in the chopper and I got out of my seat and was leaning down so I could speak to him.

'Ben, keep it all. We left it there for you, to say thanks.'

He immediately started to cry. This huge, powerful man was totally overcome with emotion and wept. He held out the gleaming spear shaft.

'No, we can't keep it. How will you feed your family when you get home?'

I smiled and slapped him on the shoulder. He was an unbelievably nice man, and a great heir to the chiefdom. It was clear that he thought our families would be at a serious disadvantage without those items, and he would not let us give them up. Obviously, he had a totally different idea of how people in our culture eat/fish/live. We took off as the huge man, having finally accepted our gifts, clutched the fins and spear to his chest and waved.

Pretty different to charity in Australia.

In Iraq I certainly experienced the extremes of heat and cold. For most of my time there I lived in a desert camp in the centre of the country, south of Baghdad. To quote an episode of *Blackadder*, it was 'a barren, featureless wasteland' on first view. Actually, even after viewing it many times, it was still a barren and featureless wasteland. At our camp, I climbed to the roof of our tallest building, three storeys, and looked all around the horizon. The only features that were of any use for navigational purposes were manmade: a tower here, a small hill from earthworks there, and a little village about a kilometre away. Nothing else really. In summer it was hot, in the low to mid 50s at times, and in the depth of winter the desert was achingly cold, below freezing with icy winds. There were also sandstorms and swarms of bugs.

I had time, while I was in Iraq, to see a certain section

of Iraqi culture pretty closely. I worked with many different Iraqis, from broadly differing ethnic and religious groups, and found this in itself highly educational. One thing that interested me greatly was the Iraqis' impressions of our culture. We taught police recruits how to conduct themselves in a democratic society and the importance of human rights, and, as an instructor, you always gave them a presentation on your home country and answered questions from the class on your own culture. This was an important way for you to build a close relationship with the students. Nearly every day for the four weeks after I gave that presentation, I would face questions about life in Australia, or other countries. Their misconceptions about the rest of the world always surprised me and it was very instructive for me to learn how we were viewed in their culture.

One day during winter, I was standing in the middle of a field training area, among some empty buildings we used for training scenarios. It was about 8 o'clock in the morning and absolutely freezing. I looked out at about 600 students, in groups of ten or so, who were meant to be making preparations for a mock attack on a set of buildings. My class was mixed in there somewhere. They didn't look like they were doing much, and I didn't blame them. As you can imagine, they didn't exactly have the latest state-of-the-art cold weather gear, and were struggling to keep warm in any way they could. I had the latest state-of-the-art cold weather gear, and I was cold. It would be idiotic to attempt to get them to crawl around and sneak into attack positions, and I was happy for them to guard themselves against the cold for a while, until the weak winter sun broke through the cloud cover. They had started about 50 or 60 little fires around the training areas, burning rubbish, or any bush they could find, and were warming their hands and faces. I wasn't going to begrudge them the tiny bit of comfort they were getting, by having them extinguish the fires and get to work.

My assigned interpreter approached me. Ali was great bloke, smart and dedicated to his job. He saw the way ahead for Iraq and wanted to be involved and do his part. He usually just stood by my side in case an Iraqi student approached me to ask a question or I needed a command passed on. We had a lot of conversations about world history and Iraqi or Australian culture, and plenty of arguments too. Many of the interpreters were scared to argue with us, as we were their bosses, but Ali and I had a great understanding, and I actually enjoyed our arguments. I respected him a great deal because of the courage he showed in arguing with me, when I had the power to sack him without redress. In Iraqi culture, you just don't argue with superiors.

I took a long look around the scene and Ali thought I was going to try to get the guys to work. He looked at me and said, 'Nathan, it is very cold for these guys. They have no coats. They are just trying to keep warm somehow.'

'Yeah, I know, Ali, but we still have work to get done.'

I wasn't trying to bait him, as I agreed, but I didn't want this to slip into a half day off for the recruits.

'Yes. You are right. It is just, you know, very cold.'

Yeah. I pulled out my notebook and wrote down some things I wanted to do later with my class and Ali looked around the field at the fires the guys had started.

'You know, Nathan. In Iraq we have a special way to keep warm, when we are in the open like this.'

He left it hanging, expectantly. I glanced up from my notebook with a look on my face that said 'Tell me more'.

'Yes. We make a fire on the ground from pieces of wood and rubbish, and all stand around it to get warm from its heat.'

First I looked at him as if he had more to add, which he did not. He looked at me to get my reaction and I thought maybe he was joking with me and I was expected to laugh. In my experience Iraqis don't have a great sense of humour, though they will tell you differently, but Ali was unusual, so maybe he had moved from historical/political debate into comedy. I waited. Nope. He obviously didn't know that standing around a fire was a universal thing and not confined to Iraq.

I raised my eyebrow at him, but still didn't know what to say. I thought about it for a second and then said, 'That's amazing, Ali. We don't really do that in Australia. Usually we just carry a couple of frogs in our pockets.'

I turned away to let him think about it and started to walk up the road. What a novel idea, starting a fire to get warm. I'm sure Ali stood there for quite a while wondering how frogs would keep you warm in such a case.

While I was in Iraq there was a big pop song that was really popular with the recruits. I won't try to write it in Arabic, but the literal translation of the words, and actual meaning, are really interesting.

SCORPION

The song is by a pop-style artist who could be likened to Justin Timberlake or whoever the latest young guy is in the West. In the video clip (which is quite an experience) he sings a sort of duet with a girl who repeats the chorus. The chorus is then sung in Arabic to each of their mothers. The chorus goes, 'Mum, I have been bitten by a scorpion!', and is repeated many times.

However, it doesn't mean that a scorpion has literally bitten either of them. Of course, it's an expression. One day, one of the interpreters was sitting next to me as I watched a large group of students dance around and sing this song, AK47 rifles held high, mimicking the cliché of Arab celebrations. (Iraq is where I learnt the expression 'celebratory gunfire'. I certainly don't know anywhere else where the two words are linked in this way.) He asked me if I knew what the song meant, and I told him that I didn't. He said, 'Well, "Mum, I have been bitten by a scorpion!" means that I have fallen in love.'

Hmmm. What a charming expression. But he wasn't really finished.

'Also, it can mean I have just been raped. Though, in this song I think it means she has fallen in love, not been raped.'

How lovely.

I was always taught to be polite and appreciative when watching a live performance. Am I wrong?

In mid-2008 I was in Burma, as part of the emergency response to the Cyclone Nargis disaster. I spent a couple of months in this politically isolated country, and got to see a side of their culture I didn't know existed, even though I had previously travelled to Burma as a tourist and had spent a bit of time around the Thai border region.

I had come in via Bangkok, and in Bangkok I teamed up with an American guy from a large, California-based NGO. This NGO is Direct Relief International and, in my opinion, is one of the best charities operating in the world. DRI was effectively paying the bills for our medical response to the disaster, so, fair enough, they wanted to have a look at what was going on.

Their representative was Matt. Now, Matt was cool. I mean, really, Matt was cool. I know plenty of people who think they are cool, and a bunch of people who do cool things, but Matt was cool. We got on really well, and had to attend a heap of meetings together. He had some good contacts that were really useful in Bangkok, and I knew some people up on the Thai/ Burma border who helped us out. He was always relaxed and dressed fashionably and comfortably and he never seemed out of place, or awkward, no matter whom we were speaking to. He was very funny and totally irreverent, especially for a human-itarian. Humanitarians, in my experience, are generally really dry and serious and always strive to be Politically Correct. To me it usually appears disingenuous. Matt wasn't like that, he was highly professional, but ready for whatever. These were all good signs. He always had a story about being backstage and hanging out with Paris Hilton, or getting drunk with some other star or the lead singer of some band. He was on it.

We had arranged sort of dodgy visas to get into Burma

through a back door, and a US State Department representative had convinced Matt that he would be arrested once he was inside. I was totally confident, but Matt was a bit stressed. In the end I convinced him that the worst that could happen was that he would be held overnight and deported the next morning. No worries. I would get a T-shirt printed up to that effect if it happened to me.

We needed these dodgy visas because the Burmese government, while telling the outside world it would accept humanitarian assistance, was in fact not letting anybody into Burma if their purpose was humanitarian aid. It was a frustrating time for the humanitarian community. We didn't want to wait for official permission, which was eventually granted months later, with many caveats attached. So, through contacts in Thailand, we obtained ten-week business visas. Mine said I was a visiting engineer consulting for a large petrochemical company. Matt's said he was a limbo dancing instructor. Just kidding.

Anyway, we got in OK. In Burma we didn't have anyone to help us out initially, so we stayed where the rest of the transient NGO community was holed up. Now, when I say holed up, I mean very comfortable in the Traders Hotel. This was a huge change for me, as on Australian Aid International projects I sleep in a tent or the cheapest place we can find. The Traders Hotel is the tallest building in Yangon, opulent, convenient and relatively expensive. I thought I would stay there for a while and then find somewhere cheaper. Traders was a focal point for the humanitarian community at the time because it was safe and undamaged, and was also the headquarters for a large UN department. I hooked back up with Matt, got the rundown on the UN schedule and what we needed to do and when, and then relaxed. Matt had wanted to go out in downtown Yangon since he got there, but didn't really have a partner in crime.

There are many beautiful and interesting cultural phenomena particular to Burma, but I'm not going to talk about any of those. I will explain some other cultural differences.

We got in a taxi and wrangled with the driver to take us to some dive. The taxi driver obviously knew better than to take a couple of foreigners down to these places, and was either reluctant or just didn't know what we were saying. Either way, we got there, to a place known as the Beer Station. It was pretty plain, with no window glass, just grills in the window frames. Inside it was dimly lit and about 200 Burmese men sat around tables that we use for outdoor furniture in Australia, roughly orientated towards a stage. Now I think that beer station is just a Burmese euphemism for bar or pub, but then we didn't really know what to expect. Matt told me that there were a bunch of girls who sing and dance on stage, and put on a fashion show, and that sounded interesting. We were the only round eyes in the place. You might think you know where this story is going, but believe me, you don't, unless you have been there.

I have travelled around South-East Asia quite a bit. When I go to a dimly lit bar, with dancing girls and singers, I know exactly what's coming: prostitutes aggressively plying their trade and a stage show that will either make you clap, cry or want to get married/divorced.

I knew this was going to be interesting on some level, even if I only judged that by the looks we were getting from the exclusively male crowd. I wasn't feeling that welcome. A waiter took us to a table close to the stage and got some drinks.

The first performer came on stage. She was a tall, attractive Burmese lady, probably about 25 years old. She was wearing a very standard T-shirt and jeans, pretty much street clothes, nothing you would imagine wearing for such a stage show.

The room went silent as she started her song, a clinky, fast-paced pop number that was either Chinese, German or Portuguese. I couldn't tell and it didn't matter.

I was shocked. It was the most joyless, sexless, monotone, drab, uninteresting, emotionless, toneless performance I had ever seen. She had a lot to learn about the stage. I felt really bad for this poor lady. When she wasn't singing she stood motionless in the centre of the stage, from which she never moved one footstep throughout the entire performance. She just stared at a point on the stage about 3 metres to her front, with a grim, sorrowful look on her face. She was like a statue, not even taking the time, while not singing, to sway her hips or tap her foot to the beat or anything. I cannot even emulate this when I try to show people how she was. I can't help it, I swing or tap my foot or something. It just happens. I challenge you to try this. Get a song you know and like, and then sing the whole thing, without moving any part of your body.

I looked around the room and everyone was watching her intently, in apparently silent contemplation. I looked across at Matt. He knew what I was thinking. Eventually, after what felt like about ten minutes, which would have seemed like excruciating torture to the woman on stage, she stopped. The crowd did nothing, utter silence. Sure, she was bad, but a little bit of encouragement never hurt anyone.

Matt and I burst into loud enthusiastic clapping and threw out a few whoops for good measure. She needed a bit of support. Well, it didn't go down too well. You could have cut the air with a knife. Nobody joined in, and at least 100 men stared at us with what looked to me like contempt.

Hmmm. OK. I was perplexed. I thought that it would have been considered polite to give her some encouragement. Everyone else in the room was unmoved. They would have been great judges for one of those talent shows on TV. They were taciturn and, really, I suppose they were right. After all, she was terrible. Fair enough, I thought. Though it goes against my general practice of at least giving her kudos for having the courage to stand up in front of an audience and sing, if not dance.

There was a group of girls gathered at a window next to the stage, the assembled singers, and they obviously appreciated the clapping, because they were standing with the singer we had just seen, beaming huge smiles at us. I assumed that they had assessed us as gentlemen for supporting the worst nightclub singer in the world.

The next girl walked out onto the stage, and the crowd silently considered her. Again, she was a tall, attractive Burmese lady, but this time she wore a long flowing dress. She looked like a seasoned performer. She launched into a similar song to the previous lady. Terrible. If I thought the last girl was bad, this one stunk. I didn't think it possible to sing a song with less emotion, but she proved me wrong. This was cruel. Again I looked around the audience and they considered her in silent critique. Imagine singing the latest Pussycat Dolls pop song and, in between verses, just standing there, perfectly still, with a frown on your face, staring straight ahead, at a crowd of 200 silent men. Weird.

As the last of the singing finished she turned to walk off stage, the only movement she had made throughout the whole act, not even waiting for the music to stop. Maybe she was going away to cry in the toilet. I hoped not.

Matt and I launched into a similarly raucous round of clapping and carrying on. Again, nobody joined in, and everyone gave us the dagger eyes. Hmmm. I looked over to the window to see all the performers crammed in to get a look at the guys clapping. All of them were beaming big smiles or giggling. Well, somebody liked us.

There was a guy sitting at the table next to us who looked about 35–40 years old. He was dressed like a local fisherman, wearing sandals, baggy pants, a sleeveless shirt and wide-brimmed hat. He stared at us coldly as the girls giggled at us warmly. I nodded and smiled at him—nothing. He just stared at me, no smile, no nod. I looked back in a second to double-check and he was still staring at me, then he mumbled something to me in Burmese, which I'm sure was meant for him to understand, not me.

OK. I looked around the room and saw that the bar staff had long multicoloured flower leis for sale. By watching the crowd for a while I worked out that the way to show appreciation for the singers was to buy one of these leis, walk up on stage and put it around her neck. This was the only act that elicited any sort of applause from the crowd. I wasn't even sure if they were clapping the singers who scored the lei or the guys who gave them out. Fair enough. So, I bought a lei to put around the neck of one of the girls.

But now we had a dilemma. It seemed to me that the girls were getting the leis from their boyfriends and husbands in the crowd, or at least from guys who really wanted to be their boyfriends and husbands. OK. I did the calculations in my head.

We are 'rich' Westerners.

The crowd hates us already.

The Fisherman looks ready to cut my throat.

The only girls in the whole place are staring at us, smiling.

I have a lei, which I am about to put around the neck of the wife or girlfriend of somebody in the room, probably The Fisherman.

Alright, so I quickly hatched a plan. I considered just giving the lei away to somebody else to hand over to one of the girls, but then that seemed a bit of a cop-out. So, I briefed Matt up. He held the same concerns as me, and, despite his international 'cool' status, was going to get his arse just as kicked as mine if the handing-over-of-the-lei ceremony went bad.

'Matt, I'm going to give this lei to the ugliest, worst-singing girl who comes on stage. As long as she's wearing the crappiest, least sexy outfit, then nobody will think I'm making a move on any of their girlfriends. Ha? What do you reckon?'

'Yep. Sounds good. But I think we better be ready to go straight after that.'

'Yep. You're right. When I stand up to give over the lei, you stand up and be ready to go for the door.'

I wanted to get out of there soon, as I could feel the crowd was pretty much over the two big round eyes getting all the looks from the singers, but there was a problem. The next girl to get on stage was gorgeous. She could sing, was beautiful and wore a long ball gown. She even betrayed a sense of rhythm by moving very slightly while she was waiting for her verses to start. No way was I marching up to her and giving her the lei. I sat tight and waited for the next singer when the next problem reared its head. The singers were having a break, and now there was going to be a quick fashion show.

This fashion show was worth seeing. It was not at all like the catwalk fashion shows I had seen on TV. Firstly, all the models came on stage at once, about eight at a time, and then they did a sort of walking-pace dance routine, moving about the stage in loosely choreographed moves that were almost like military drill. On their faces were the, now typical, expression-less masks of Burmese stage performers, or, if they were really seasoned performers, the sort of sad expression that made them look like they were thinking about puppies being euthanised. The piece de resistance was that they all wore identical dresses. Usually they were long ball gowns in garish colours, similar to what bridesmaids wore in Australia in the mid 1980s. Nice.

Well, Matt and I sat through this performance, and gave our now ubiquitous clap at the end. Why stop now? Mercifully, the singers came on and I got my chance to offload my lei. The first girl was no good. Way too young and attractive. The next girl was perfect. Dowdy, expressionless, terrible singer, no dance moves—perfect. She was my girl. I had to get her before she raced off the stage at the end of her last verse, as I knew she wouldn't stick around until the end of the song, but the problem was that I didn't have a clue when that was.

CUP OF TEA

How could I judge when the last verse had ended? Towards the end of the song I made my move. I stood up, winked at The Fisherman and walked up on stage. The girl was stunned. She looked like she was going to faint, and then smiled, weakly. She looked at the lei in my hand and bowed slightly. I shook her hand, put the lei around her neck, did a snappy turn, and acknowledged the muted clapping from the crowd.

Matt was standing next to the table and gestured towards the door. Yep, we were out of there. I walked straight past The Fisherman and he stared at me but I could read what his face said, 'Keep walking, Round Eye.'

So, yeah. File that one away for if you ever find yourself in a beer station in Yangon.

Also, next time I'm back home and sitting through a really crappy performance, I'm not clapping or moving a muscle at the end. As a culturally broadened person, that's now my right.

I'll let you know how it goes.

I have observed many cultures where following a process dogmatically is more important than actually doing the thing that the process serves. Like if you have a certain process for making a cup of tea for a guest where you do as follows:

Put teabag in cup.

Put water in kettle and turn on.

Three minutes later pour water from kettle into cup.

Jiggle teabag for one minute then remove.

Give tea to guest.

OK, so that's the intended process for making the tea. But what if, at point 2 there's a power outage and the water doesn't boil? Well, in some cultures that rely heavily on processes, you just carry on and present the cold cup of tea to the guest. Was the tea made? No. Was the process followed? Yes. The process is important so everything is OK.

This culture may not be confined to a nation, or ethnic group, but perhaps a corporate group, or community of some type. In a way I actually like it, because it allows me to exactly predict what another person will do in a given situation. This is rare and important knowledge.

In Iraq at one point I was working as a security contractor, driving around in armoured vehicles. It's a strange existence working as a security operator in a place like that. It's easy, and operationally sound, to see yourself as under siege, in danger every time you step outside your fortified encampment. You see the enemy in every person you observe. This can be very hard for some people. You need a lot of attributes to be good at that job. It is a strange mix of being calm and restrained but being a great marksman. I have always argued that we can teach anyone to be a good marksman, so you need to recruit a relaxed, confident guy, rather than a dead-eye-dick shot. If a person is not culturally sensitive and relaxed in his surroundings, then it will be pretty hard to instil that. Shooting skills are easy by comparison. Part of that necessary cultural sensitivity is recognising people's reliance on procedures.

One particular day we arrive at the Baghdad International Airport to pick up some incoming passengers, to transport them to the Green Zone in Baghdad.

CIVILIAN CARS

At the airport at this stage, our vehicles, and we ourselves, have to go through a security check. All civilian vehicles (which we technically are, according to the process) must pass through the same check, before they are allowed to continue on towards the airport.

Many civilian cars are stopped in front of us, being searched for weapons and bombs, so we wait. In our convoy are three Toyota Landcruisers, all obviously private security detachment vehicles. We have eleven personnel with us, all security contractors decked out with rifles, pistols, machine guns, grenades, Kevlar helmets, ten magazines of bullets for each rifle, body armour, radios, etc. We are very clearly a security detachment going to the airport to pick up clients.

Our cars are conspicuously armoured, and adorned with flashing lights, flags and signs in Arabic asking people to keep back, spotlights, ramming bars, recovery and communications gear, GPS receivers and bristling with guns. In the cars are mounted Mag 58 machine guns, at least 5000 rounds for each gun, ten smoke grenades, ten flares and about five grenades. We could fight a little war, if need be.

We get to the front of the queue and the searchers come forward. They are armed, but not anywhere near as heavily as us. Each crew member gets out of the car carrying all his personal weapons, and leaves the doors open. We stand aside and the searchers walk up to the cars. They look under front seats, and in the foot wells, poke around in the back where the machine gun is mounted and the compartment is literally filled with bombs and bullets. They open the bonnet and look at the engine compartment. When one of the searchers comes close to me I say, 'Hey mate, what are you looking for?'

'Guns and bombs. Please stand back.'

Hmmm, OK. I think to myself, well, I would say you have found them. Each of us has two to three guns and plenty of bombs.

After a minute the searcher gives us the thumbs-up and says, 'OK. You can go in.'

He waves at the guards ahead to let them know we are OK.

Process says, Search all vehicles for guns and bombs. Process served. I love it.

I was out on the roads on another day, and was the second in charge of our crew. The team leader was in the rear vehicle, and I was in the front vehicle, in the front passenger seat. It was my job to commentate on the radio about everything I could see to my front and sides and get our vehicle to pave the way for the whole convoy.

We come up to some slow-moving traffic and keep a polite (safe) distance. Our main threat comes from suicide bombers in cars, so slowing down and getting stuck in traffic makes everyone nervous. Especially the occupants of the other cars on the road, who generally don't want to be anywhere near us, for good reason.

We push through to the front of the traffic blockage and form a rough protective shape on a clear piece of road, covering all sides.

Ahead I can see three dark-coloured sedans speeding

towards us. I alert everyone on the radio.

'This is Zulu 1. Three dark fast movers approaching. Stand-by.'

In this case standby means be alert but don't take any action.

I open my door slightly, swing my rifle out and look down my magnified scope to get a better look. However, I know this move will make all the other team members think I'm about to shoot somebody, and therefore adopt a similar position. I don't want that. Everyone else just needs to sit tight. So I commentate on the radio.

'Zulu 1 just looking guys. Standby.'

Down my scope I can see some males hanging out of the rear windows of the second sedan. The cars all seem to have white Arabic writing on the doors. Is this a militia hit squad? I can't tell.

The team leader is in the car furthest from the action, and he wants to know what's going on. The dark sedans are totally ignoring our sirens and flashing lights and are still heading towards us at great speed. The team leader speaks over the radio. 'What's happening with those fast movers, Nathan?'

'Standby, Zulu 3.'

It's one of those moments. Do I start shooting to stop their approach? If I start shooting everyone in the team will. But it doesn't feel like an attack. In my mind I list what I can deduce about the situation.

They aren't positioning their vehicles in the right way to hit us.

The guys hanging out the windows are not going to be very effective shooters.

They are driving erratically, not in a determined way.

We constitute a difficult, dispersed target.

Surely, this can't be an attack.

I quickly look left and right around the area and try to think of what our next move will be if they do open fire or detonate a bomb. Where can we move our vehicle to? Where are the rest of our vehicles in relation to my vehicle? Has anyone moved position? Where are our vehicles with heavy machine guns onboard? Which way are they oriented?

The cars are getting pretty close now. My driver cracks his door open and swings his rifle out too. That's OK with me, he's calm and cool, but the rest of the team in the other vehicles may see this as an escalation. I come up on the radio again, interrupting somebody about to talk, probably the team leader asking for an update. I speak deliberately and calmly.

'This is Zulu 1. All call signs, wait, wait.'

In radio speak this means get off the radio so it's clear for me to say anything I need to say urgently, and literally, wait.

If there needs to be any shooting done, I want the least amount of rounds fired, so it's best if just my driver and I shoot. I look down my scope and say to the driver, 'Hang on a bit longer, mate. It doesn't feel like a threat.'

He replies, 'No worries, Nath.'

It's go time. I flick my safety catch off and hear the driver do the same. Then I see it. It's an Iraqi wedding party.

'Zulu 1! All call signs stand down. It's a wedding party.'

We'd held off so long we had put ourselves in some danger. But it was worth it.

They drive past honking their horns and singing.

So, if you're planning a wedding in Baghdad, remember to make allowances for driving around erratically with your friends and relatives hanging out the windows and totally ignoring the guys with the armoured vehicles who are about to open fire. I wonder if wedding planners in Baghdad factor that in.

I have filed that away for next time.

The whole incident, start to finish, probably took eight seconds. In those eight seconds we had so many critical decisions to make. We were calm, confident, reserved and trusted each other.

But what if we weren't? What if we were tired and trying to work the radios in two different languages, uncertain of our weapons and unconfident in our marksmanship? What if we were 18-years-olds, led by a 20-year-old who looked like an extra from *She Got Game* or some other teen film? What if we were lowly paid and going to be in this hellhole for fourteen months before we could go home? What if we had already been attacked that week, or that day? How would our confidence be? What if three of our mates had been killed? How would our decision-making abilities be then?

Well, that's the reality for every US service-person working in Iraq. I will ask another question. How do any of them get home without psychological problems?

What a place.

This story isn't really about the Iraqi culture and how they celebrate weddings. It's about the culture of the Australian private security detachment I worked with and it's about the culture of the American soldiers working in that place, and what their culture makes them contend with every day.

DECISIONS

They make mistakes, I agree. I shake my head and feel disgust when I see some of their decisions, but don't be too quick to judge them. I'm not anymore.

CHAPTER 11

There is no such thing as bad conditions,
only bad equipment

'Check my back!'

'Check my back!' This is what we yell during military para-chuting as we're about to jump out of the plane. It's the last in a long line of checks that your parachute and equipment have undergone before you actually use them. We stand in single file doing most of the checking but the last guy in line has nobody to check his back, of course. So when all the checking is done, we all yell 'Check my back!' and turn around on the spot. Of course, only the last guy's parachute needs to be checked, because everyone else already had somebody behind him. We still ALL yell the same thing though, so there can be no mistakes.

Your parachute has been checked many times before this, but it is always worth checking again. It gets checked when it is manufactured. It gets checked when it gets packed. Then, when the parachutist picks up the parachute he's going to use, he checks it as well. You put on the parachute, check it again, then get your mate to check it, then a supervisor checks it again. Then you get in the plane and check it again, the supervisor checks again and we yell 'Check my back!' and you know the rest. It's a good system. No mistakes. You don't get second chances parachuting from 1000 feet/300 metres.

I loved that about the army. You don't feel stupid checking something that you know has just been inspected, you're commanded to do it, and that's all there is to it. There is a reliability of action to this, too. I know, when I get to the plane, that at least three separate pairs of eyes have given my equipment the nod and I'm ready to go. Trust is there too. I can't do the final check on my parachute, because it's an inspection of the back section, and I'm already wearing it. It doesn't worry me though, because I know, absolutely, that my mate behind me has scrutinised it the same way he would check his own.

Of course this level of caution is over the top, but my point is that you need to check your equipment. The more critical or potentially dangerous the equipment, the more it needs to be checked. You need to make sure you have a good understanding of its operation and what to do if it doesn't work the way you were expecting.

Also, your new solar laptop/satellite phone charger will always work when you test it in the backyard, instruction manual in one hand, in bright sunshine on a beautiful summer's day. Will it work after having been in the bottom of your pack for two weeks, when you need it to work NOW, in the rain, while 200 local villagers watch? Not likely.

Australian Aid International supports a number of projects up on the Thai/Burma border. We're a bunch of military-trained medics, and the guys we work with up there are a bunch of field medics running around in the jungle treating gunshot and mine injuries. Exactly what military medics do.

GENERALISATIONS

Doctors are not medics, and medics are not doctors. Medics generally deal in unsanitary, unsavoury conditions, performing surgery on the school bench or in the back of a truck. Medics work from their packs, and usually don't have an assistant to help. Doctors are generally much more knowledgeable but crave a nice white sheet and beautifully presented operating room. Of course these are generalisations, but I'm just trying to point out that their perspectives are different. There are many important operational skills that medics can teach doctors, but expert doctors are also there to teach and advise, and we don't have a program without their help.

At the beginning of 2008 I was up there working with Frank, Dom and some others from AAI. We were running a medic's course and had a number of excellent doctors on the training staff. Dom is a friend from the army, who was also a police officer. He has no medical skills but was there to write a report, gather information and generally help in administration. Running this course is quite a feat of coordination, as we bring staff from all around the world, and students, who make a perilous trip, from deep inside Burma.

We usually get around the town on small motorbikes, just like the locals. These bikes are easy to ride, don't have a clutch, but do have manual gears. I remember Frank throwing Dom the keys to one of our bikes and asking, 'Are you sure you know how to ride a motorbike?'

Dom looked quite offended and gave him the 'Of course' face, shook his head and said, 'Yeah. What do you reckon?'

OK, fair enough. Frank and I were experienced and licensed motorcycle riders from back home, and had both ridden motorbikes in more countries than we could remember. We didn't give it another thought.

We had an eminent orthopaedic surgeon from the US helping us for this course. She was about 45 years old, and one of the best in her field. We were looking after her as well as we could, in the circumstances. She had not worked with AAI before, and maybe we seemed to be a bit high speed for her style.

Dom had been riding the bikes without incident for a few days and was tasked with transporting the surgeon a couple of kilometres to the medical school we had set up. The school is a basic set of rooms with desks and chairs for the students, projectors, computers, medical training aids and a few textbooks. It was simple, but fit for the purpose.

Anyway, the surgeon got on the back of the bike as Dom donned his cheap plastic motorcycle helmet that looked like a child's toy. He revved the bike up but it stalled as he tried to take off. He tried again with a few more revs, with the same result. He needed to hold a bit of front brake on, rev it up then let the front brake off slowly to affect a good start. We soon found out he didn't know this.

He put the little motorbike in neutral, revved it right up and then slammed the gear level into first gear—with predictable results. Before anyone could stop him the bike did a beautiful wheelie towards the road, dumped the highly paid surgeon on her bum on the concrete and took off like a rearing stallion. Oh shit. At least she was an established expert on broken bones. We might need her advice. Her hands were probably insured for a million dollars. This wasn't good. Dom was now dancing around not knowing quite what to do, and Frank was ready to kill somebody. Well, not somebody—Dom.

We picked her up and she was a little bit bruised and battered, but OK. To her immense credit, she was wonderful about the whole incident. Brushed it off like it was nothing. Nice lady, terrific instructor, skilled surgeon—and not the lawsuit type!

The next day she was wearing a bandage and every time Frank saw the bandage he muttered something about Dom under his breath. Classic. If she hadn't already been wearing the bandage, I would have begged her to put one on, just so people would ask what happened. That way we could point to Dom/Evel Knievel and his trick motorcycling skills.

Dom has a lot of great qualities. He is charming, intelligent, diligent, a great team member and an excellent friend. He is also over-confident. Lots of guys I know are, and I'm not going to throw too many stones there myself.

The incident blew over and a few days later I was sitting with Frank, writing a report on my laptop, when Dom walked in. He asked me for the keys to my bike. He had never ridden my motorcycle before. I looked at Frank, he muttered something unrepeatable and I shot a smart-arse smile at Dom who said, 'Hurry up.' And gave me a dismissive look like, 'Yeah, yeah, just give me the keys.'

He was in a hurry and I handed over the keys but I couldn't resist.

'Are you sure you know how to ride a motorbike?'

He shook his head wearily and stomped out.

Strangely, he walked back in a minute later and handed over my keys.

'The battery's dead on your bike.'

I found this strange. 'How do you know?'

He gave me that look again, and said, 'I pressed the button and it doesn't turn over.'

'It has no electric start, Dom. It has a kick-starter. Have you heard of them? Yeah, you know how to ride a motorbike.'

Classic. I couldn't stop laughing for about twenty minutes. Dom's confidence had taken a thorough beating, and needed it.

Dom's mistake was he didn't know his equipment, mine was not paying attention, the surgeon's was trusting Dom.

When you first join the commandos you have to do an amphibious operations course. I loved every minute of it. It was hard and you were freezing cold every day, and worked really long hours carrying heavy boats or swimming in the cold Southern Ocean, but I enjoyed it. As a surfer I was used to the cold and felt comfortable in the ocean. Some guys were really scared of being in the ocean at night and hadn't been really cold in their entire lives.

Before you can learn to use the boats you have to know how to use your safety gear. That would be your flares, personal flotation device, strobe and fins. That way, even if you get into trouble during your first time on the boats, you can save yourself.

A guy called Squizzy was our instructor for the lesson on flares. He was very serious, and was a 'respect my authority' type, even though he was actually a mechanic in the army, and not an actual commando.

After the instruction there was always a demonstration of

how the safety equipment worked. In this case it was the day/night flare.

Squizzy held the flare in one hand and unscrewed the safety cap. He put his finger under the ignition ring and got ready to ignite the flare. He said, 'It's very important to really get a good hold on the ring, so you can yank it hard just once.'

He pulled the ring and it came off in his hand. Just like in a cartoon, he took a look at the end where the ring broke. On cue, the flare ignited in his face.

Boom!

Once the smoke cleared Squizzy was sort of staggering around, a bit shaken, but unhurt. He had now totally taken on a cartoon persona. He was swaying and coughing out little clouds of smoke and his hair was all spiky like a mad scientist's. His face was blackened and his sunglasses sat sideways across his face. He was speechless, for once.

It was hard, I mean really hard, to keep from laughing—so I didn't bother trying.

One night, while I was a police officer, I got asked to go out on patrol with the supervising sergeant. He was a great guy, very energetic and had a good sense of humour. It was a Friday night, and he wanted to have a look through the pubs in our area and make sure there was no trouble.

We had only been out of the office about ten minutes and a job came over the police radio. There was a break-in at a local factory and the silent alarm was going off. It was very close to where we were so I drove there at breakneck speed. Now, most sergeants are pretty happy to sit back and let other people run into the fight/fire/domestic/robbery etc. but not this guy. He was jumping out of his skin and just about frothing at the mouth to get into the action. I admired that. He had been around for twenty years or so, and was still keen.

He leapt out of the car as we pulled up at the factory gates and ran over to the fence. I stopped the car, got out and ran after him. He decided to give me some words of advice.

'Mate, be ready for anything. Who knows what these bastards are up to? Have your gun ready when we get over the fence, and make sure your gear is ready for the climb.'

He was obviously preparing for the worst, which is a good policy. He also obviously thought he needed to remind me to check my equipment before going into the danger area. Also a good policy. I had a feel around my equipment belt to make sure everything was in place. He wanted to go over first so I gave him a boost, but the fence was very high. I reached up so he could brace his feet against my hands and I could push him up higher and over the top. I would climb over later.

He wasn't making very fast progress and I looked up to see him in a contorted position with one leg up on top of the fence and then I noticed something very significant. His revolver was sliding out of its holster. I yelled, 'Your gun!'

Actually, I only got 'Your' out before a Smith and Wesson Model 10, κ Frame .38 Special hit me in the forehead and bounced onto the ground.

The sergeant was always full of good advice, taking his own advice was another matter.

GOOD ADVICE

Things happen and mistakes are made. We should try to cut those mistakes down to a minimum though. My first boss, Bruce, used to say, 'The man who never made a mistake never made anything.'

Good advice, but I would also say, 'The man who makes the same mistake again and again is as useless as a chocolate teapot.'

A few weeks after the gun-to-the-head incident described above, I was at the office. The same sergeant was on duty. The alarm went off at the bank about 100 metres from the police station. This could be a goer. This is why we joined the police and we were on it. We both raced out the door at a sprint to see what was going on. Everything looked OK from outside and we slowed down to assess the scene. These days, if you want to rob a bank, you use a gun, so I was ready for anything, but didn't want to rush in and get shot. I unclipped the safety bar on my holster and lifted my revolver out an inch or two, then replaced it, leaving the safety bar unclipped. This made me confident that I could draw it quickly.

I looked across at the sergeant and he was fumbling around at his holster. Then I saw him look down at his equipment belt and heard him utter a muted, 'Shit!'

I had a good look at his holster. No gun. He had not put a gun in his belt at the beginning of his shift, thinking he was going to be doing paperwork all day, and it slipped his mind as he ran out.

REALITY

He was going to a gunfight with no gun. Nice one. I turned my attention back to the bank, and we started to close in. To his credit (maybe) he didn't slow down and was there as we approached the doors.

I took the lead at the doors and looked in. Everything seemed like business as usual, because it was. False alarm. Very lucky for Sergeant No-Gun anyway.

I have made light of this situation, because I can. Nobody got hurt and everyone walked away laughing in the end. These sorts of small but significant mistakes can have tragic consequences. I have used the examples above from my police career because the mistakes were not made by some sort of bumbling Inspector Clouseau character. They were made by one of the better police officers I know, and a man I would happily stand next to in the worst of situations. In reality, if it can happen to him, it can happen to anybody. This is the very reason the army demand that your parachute is checked and re-checked.

Also, even knowing that he had no gun, he was willing to approach the bank where we believed an armed robbery was in progress. That's an impressive act of bravery, in my book.

I said at the start of this book that I'm not educated, but I'm experienced. I can tell you that a lot of that experience was in making mistakes. At various times I have forgotten everything that was not stitched onto me and exploded many things that I could have sworn were absolutely inert and impossible to ignite. Some of those incidents confound teams of scientists to this day. I have broken, crashed, fallen, vomited and otherwise offended or nearly killed people in an ever-increasing number of countries, all in the name of helping. My section in the military received a lifetime ban from our commanders on the sport of Hacky Sack/foot bag because of all the injuries we induced. That game was invented as a low-impact form of recovery from injury! I have had to whisper 'I think we better leave' so many times that one of my mates now instinctively ducks every time he hears that expression. It's like a nervous affliction for him. I say 'Possessions are fleeting' in response to breakages/losses so often that people think I'm some sort of Buddhist monk, on a quest for an uncluttered life. Oh, and don't sneak up behind me at night, anything could happen.

Knowing your equipment is relative. For a person surviving in the jungle, his or her equipment might be a stick, a rock and some leaves you can eat. You still have to know what to eat and what to discard though.

I was doing some survival training with the Singaporean commandos in a training centre in Singapore. We only had a knife and a water bottle for the training, so the equipment we had to get familiar with was whatever we could find in the jungle. Now, Singapore is pretty small, and if you get lost in Singapore and are in a survival situation, I think you should just walk to the local 7-Eleven and call a taxi. Have an ice-cream while you wait. You really can't go far on that island. Be that as it may, they have some excellent jungle survival instructors there, and their lessons are good for any jungle environment.

Our instructor was teaching us to recognise different plants and animals so we could identify what was a good source of nutrition and what was poisonous. It was good training, interesting and enjoyable.

The instructor was a little Singaporean-Malay guy with a huge moustache like Groucho Marx. I'm not even sure that it was real. He was funny and very knowledgeable about the jungle in general.

Near the end of his lesson he passed around pieces of fruit to all the students and asked everyone to listen to him before eating it. He asked everyone to smell it. It had quite a rich, sweet smell. This was going to be our dessert. Nice.

On cue he then got everyone to stick it straight in their mouths and start chewing fast. After about three seconds it gave off the worst taste I have ever been assaulted by. I looked around and there were Aussie soldiers everywhere gagging and spitting out this disgusting fruit and trying to scrape the taste off their tongues.

We all looked at him standing in the centre of the circle as he quietly giggled.

'The lesson here is, don't get lost in the jungle, or you end up eating crap like that!'

Nice one.

CHAPTER 12

You got this far, now the easy bit

**'Please remove your headsets
and hand them to the flight attendants.'**

Ok, firstly, if you did buy the book as an instructional manual for amputating a leg, then sorry, you were duped. In that case, I do have a few recommendations though. You should read *Where There Is No Doctor*. That book is a guide for people in remote areas or humanitarians working with injured people in disasters. It has really simple explanations and pictures and is the sort of book MacGyver would have loved, had he ever needed to do surgery. Of course, there is the horror scenario of people reading *Where There Is No Doctor* and then practising quackery at home. In that case I reckon there is only one more cringe-inducing book in the whole world, and that is *Where There Is No Dentist*. I have seen it on bookshelves but have frankly been too afraid to open it. It sounds like a torture manual to me.

I swear, this is the last time, but my legal team has absolutely demanded that I tell you not to buy those books so you can amputate legs or practise any other home surgery at all, for fun, profit, or otherwise.

Actually, those are two excellent books, when read and used responsibly. But, I digress.

I'm not sure this book should have a conclusion in the traditional sense. I have not made any contentions that I need to revisit and somehow claim are now proved. I can't do that. I have opinions and stories to illustrate why I came up with those opinions and nothing more solid than that. Please draw your own conclusion about the book, as you should about all things.

I hope the book has entertained you, but actually, I hope I have snuck a bit of advice in there too. The sorts of things I reckon you can take from each chapter were probably clear at the time. Be calm, manage your fears, pay attention, make sure you know how to use that new piece of equipment, keep your sense of humour. Also, don't explode your rubbish, nobody will like it.

But there is an overriding message I would want you to take away. That is the importance of community service. If you are reading this book, you are rich. I know you don't feel rich, but you are. On a global scale you are particularly fortunate. I don't begrudge people that good fortune, but I reckon we can be better at recognising it, and giving some back.

I would like to encourage people to have a good look at the circumstances facing the world and see what they can do about it. You don't need to throw your job in and go to Goma to help with the humanitarian crisis, and I'm not talking here about making a donation, but look for a way you might be able to volunteer your time or effort for a charity of some sort.

At Australian Aid International we do this high-end version of humanitarianism that involves flying to exotic locations with your friends and dealing with the issues you see on the world news. You see the drama of the world in turmoil—war, famine and all manner of natural disasters—and get your hands stained with blood saving people's lives. Then you come back and get accolades and back-slapping, awards, guest speaker positions and media interviews.

At the end of the day though, it is not the people like me I admire. We do the easy bit. We do the glamour bit. We do the exciting bit. We get to author books and hold court at dinner parties. But there are heroes around us.

I admire the people who grind away at their charitable endeavours every single day. Year in, year out, often thanklessly. I know a woman who fosters profoundly disabled, extremely dependent children, and has for years. Because of their medical conditions, she has had to endure the premature deaths of these children way too often and stoically keeps acting out of love for these kids. I can honestly say that her bravery embarrasses me and every supposed tough guy I know. She will never author a book, walk on stage to be venerated, or receive monetary compensation anywhere near the value of the work she has been doing for years. She is doing that work for the kids, and for us. In saying all this, she is not embittered or angry, she is happy and charming and always cheerful. She is a hero, and a much better example than I for a charitable ideology.

I'm not saying that you need to emulate her, because I know that is close to an impossible task. But we can find places for our charitable endeavours, where others can show us the way. Once you start looking you will find that these caring people are everywhere. They work in homeless shelters, halfway houses and refugee centres. They make soup and drive around delivering it to homeless people at nights. They walk the streets and find the people whose lives are lost. I know of a computer-based system where designers, lawyers, account-ants, project managers and administrative assistants download a task to complete and return by a certain date. The tasks have been put on the system by not-for-profit agencies that can't hire a professional to do these jobs. They get the job, do it and return it without ever having contact with the agency, without getting a thank-you card or having any way to see how the project develops. They do as many jobs as they like. There is no payment and no accolades for them, they just do it. They don't even get that team feeling of accomplishment or cama-raderie. There are no high fives with their team-mates when a project goes well. They are anonymous, and only identified by a code number or name. But they do it. It is a highly suc-cessful network that takes advantage of the fact that people in the modern world might be time poor but still willing to help. I reckon that's inspirational.

They might do this work every day, one night a week or one day a month, but they are there, and we need them. How many of us can honestly claim that they cannot afford one day a month to help a charity?

These places are full of special people and experiences and I implore you to help if you can.

If you still think the sort of work I do is inspirational, then take heart. I have done all the things spelled out in the chapters you have just read while being married, having kids, a normal car, a mortgage and all the trappings of modern life in Australia.

KNOWLEDGE

I am not Rambo, Mother Teresa or Walker, Texas Ranger, or any combination of the three. Nobody is—not even Rambo, Mother Teresa and Walker, Texas Ranger. Plenty of people have told me they would love to go out and do humanitarian work, but have a cat or a goldfish or whatever, and therefore can't. Frank would sarcastically tell those people that somebody needs to rearrange those sock drawers, and that may be them. If you want to dive in, do it. It does take a commitment from your family, and I will always be thankful for the support I get from my own, but have a go. It is all there waiting for you.

The age of the internet should have another effect on us. It can bring us closer and inform us better than ever before about what is going on in the world. We need to develop that kinship with others more now than we have ever needed to. The potential destructive forces in the world are far more efficient now than they ever have been, but knowledge of our fellow humans and the up-to-the-minute information that is available to us, should counteract that.

When I was about to leave Bougainville in 2000, Joseph, a rebel commander, was saying goodbye and thanking my contingent for taking the time and effort to leave their homes far away to come and help secure peace on his tiny island home. He marvelled that the small and large nations of the Pacific made the effort to send troops for a peaceful purpose to Bougainville and he was glad to have help from people in his region. He used a Tok Pisin phrase for the kinship he felt existed between these nations, and I will never forget it. He said we were all 'Brata belong won solwara'.

Literally, this means we are brothers that belong to one

saltwater and the translation means we are related by living in the same ocean. I have always found this to be a beautifully simple way to express the kinship that relates all people in a region.

So go out, meet your brata belong won solwara and learn about them and yourself. Watch out for white-tailed spiders, though.

Thanks. Good luck and keep your head down.

Nathan Mullins

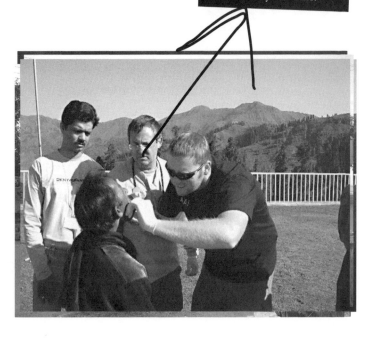

THANKS MATE

Sir Isaac Newton said:
if I have seen further it is only by standing
on the shoulders of Giants.'

Here is the list of Giants
on whose shoulders I must regularly stand.

Frank Mullins, and all the family, Campbell Burnet and family, Craig Esposito, Paul Piaia and all the family, Frank and Marina Tyler, Al Cooke and family, Dom Bowen, the Lalande family, Paul Reardon, Gav Humphries, Angelica Fleischer, the McDowall family, Dave Harmer, Pete Korszla, Pat Veitch and family, Larry Stock, Dutchie 'the Duke' Van Der Heyden, Dave Millar, Rob Heip, Danny Durovic, Anthony Oliver, Johnny Lewis, Paul Hansen and the other stars of the book, Vince, Chris, Silas, Matt MacCalla, Kahlia, Ehaka, Tim, Joseph, Todd Robinson, Dodge, Schippy, Ali, Jim Hardy, Pete Korszla, John Whykes, John Vereker and the Australian Defence Force, Victoria Police, Australian Aid International and the whole cast of the Burmese Beer Station Dance/Singing Concert and Fashion Show.

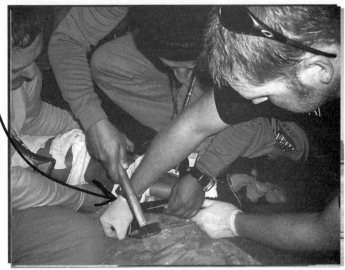

I told you – that's it.